The little "superhero" on the cover is Andrew Smith. Andrew was a bright, energetic, perfectly healthy twenty-one-month-old child when it was discovered that a virus was rapidly destroying his liver. Five days later, he had his first liver transplant. As it turned out, he needed three liver transplants in thirteen months. Against all odds, through the mercy of God and the continued prayers of many, he has survived and recovered; as one doctor put it, "beyond my wildest prayers."

Andrew is now five and has endured much with remarkable courage throughout most of his short life. He still has some challenges, but he is able to enjoy kicking a ball, riding his bike and playing with friends. He has a good sense of humour and is full of imagination and caring for others. Given the trauma he has endured, that is one of the greatest miracles. This outfit was given to Andrew by a family member as a symbol of the supernatural strength God has given him

"I picked up my copy of *Naturally Supernatural* and was literally unable to lay it down. It immediately touched something deep in my heart. Gary has captured the ethos and kingdom sensitivity that has been such a vital part of our movement. He has always been a master craftsman in communicating on vital issues. But this is Gary at his best, presenting the kingdom at its best."
Bert Waggoner – National Director, Vineyard Churches USA

"Want to know what following Jesus looks like today? Then read this book! I found it a riveting read – clearly articulated, unforgettable, vivid stories and immensely practical. Gary hits the nail on the head with this one! It is not only a 'must read' book, but also a 'must do'!"
John Mumford – National Director, Vineyard Churches UK

"Everyone seems to 'understand' that life after death is taken care of by believing in Jesus. But very few people have a vision or imagination for a Jesus-inspired, eternal kind of life now. Such a 'now-life' is derived from and lived in the kingdom of God. Gary Best knows where to find this life and points us to it with clarity of thought and easy readability. Read *Naturally Supernatural* and follow Gary into a different kind of life – the 'with-God' life most of us have dreamed of having."
Todd Hunter – President, Alpha USA

"*Naturally Supernatural* is two great things rolled into one: On-fire theology and a fantastic story. Christendom owes a great debt to Gary Best for faithfully following the Lord

where few others have dared to go, and then calling out to the rest of us, 'Come on in, the water's fine!' Read this book and enjoy getting your feet wet – or why not get all wet? – in the miraculous good news."
Mike Mason – bestselling author of *The Mystery of Marriage*, *Practicing the Presence of People* and *Champagne for the Soul*

"I believe Gary Best has been given a unique and specific gift of teaching that is for the strengthening of the body of Christ. In turbulent times, marked by swings of the pendulum, Gary charts a unifying course through what some consider controversial topics and leaves you longing for more of the living God and his wonderful Holy Spirit."
Brent Cantelon – Senior Pastor, Christian Life Assembly, Langley, BC, Canada

"Widely illustrated with present-day stories, Gary's book brings heaven to earth and shows that Jesus makes the supernatural natural for all believers, even today."
Jackie Pullinger-To – St. Stephen's Society Hong Kong

"This book is amazing – I love the blend of stories and biblical teaching. It's such an inspiring and clear call to all of us 'normal' people to life in the kingdom of God!"
Brian Doerksen – Worship leader and recording artist

NATURALLY SUPERNATURAL
JOINING GOD IN HIS WORK

GARY BEST

Vineyard International Publishing
PO Box 53286
Kenilworth 7745
Cape Town
South Africa
Email: vip@vineyardbi.org

First published 2005
Reprinted 2006, 2008

Cover photograph Jon Best, Canada
Cover design by Jon Best and Mercy Arts Studio, USA

ISBN 0-620-34814-3

CONTENTS

ACKNOWLEDGEMENTS

None of our journeys is independent; many who have gone before us have helped to bring greater potential to our path through their faithfulness. I am so thankful for my mom and dad, Eric and Gertie Best, who faithfully over many years have modelled for me the central importance of the Great Commandment and the truth of Jesus' words: "It is more blessed to give than to receive." I will be forever grateful for the spiritual parenting that John and Carol Wimber provided for Joy and me, making room in their lives for an inexperienced but eager young couple from the hinterland of Canada. John freely gave me not only his mind, but also his heart. It has changed the course of my life.

No one has done more to help me stay on course in pursuit of the kingdom and all its manifestations than my wife Joy. Her passion and zeal to see God's rule break through into our lives inspires me and motivates me in our more discouraging times. Our children, Jon and Jaana, and our son-in-law Jeremy have blessed and challenged us with the authenticity of their wholehearted pursuit of a genuine relationship with God. I often say that I have learned as much from them as I have taught them.

God has graciously given me special friends along the way who have significantly formed and encouraged me. Brent Rue (now with Jesus) and Blaine Cook tirelessly answered my incessant questions in the early days and especially taught me to spell faith, R-I-S-K. Blaine made a place for me. I will never forget it. Peter Davids, a long-term friend and former coworker, has kept me from unintentional heresy. He lent his brilliant mind and tender heart to the process of forming this manuscript. Other, more recent friends, such as Joyce Heron and Katherine Bentham have convinced me that the values I write about have truly become rooted in the next generation. This gives me great joy!

I am especially grateful to Suzie Watts for creating a draft manuscript out of spoken versions of this material, enabling me to have a guide to write from. Monique Tute, a coworker at Vineyard Resource Canada, graciously added editing expertise as well as assisting Joy in producing the study material that follows each chapter. My thanks are owed to Jon, our firstborn, for his creative touch in editing, graphics and layout. He definitely has his mother's eye! I am also grateful for Kim Hough and Rhonda Crouse at VIP. Kim's patience and energy helped tremendously to bring this all together in its final stages and Rhonda provided many constructive final editing suggestions. Stephan Vosloo added his expertise to the final cover design. Thank you also to Dave and Brenda Smith and their little superhero Andrew.

Finally, I want to thank my friend, Derek Morphew, for his vision to see this project through to conclusion. This book exists because of his belief in the importance of helping "everyone to play" and his relentless prodding over the last several years to have me write about it. He repeatedly countered my hesitations (Shouldn't you write once you have something truly significant to say?) with the firm conviction that the present need for the message of this book outweighs any inadequacy on my part. I only hope that he is right.

Respectfully,
Gary Best

FOREWORD

BY CAROL WIMBER

I think we were in Holland visiting a new church plant and John was sitting with me for a change. (I'm not bitter!) He wasn't speaking … just a part of the congregation that morning, enjoying the church and the time together. Gary was teaching and I noticed how John's attention was riveted on what Gary was saying. He always listened intently to whoever was teaching, but this was different. From relaxed contemplation, he was suddenly so serious. Gary taught and it was wonderful. So simple, so clear. My thoughts at the time were, "Oh, I've got to remember this! This is what the Vineyard is! This is what John has been saying!" I turned to John, "He's got it, John … it's all in there, in his spirit. And boy, can he say it!"

John's reply was something like, "I know, Carol. He says it all so clearly, but he needs to write it down. He communicates the Vineyard, the kingdom and the values better than I do. He needs to write that book."

I don't remember if we got to talk to Gary after the service that day, but it was on John's mind and I know John and Gary did spend time together over the next few years. As a matter of fact, the conference he did for Gary in late

1997 was the last time John went anywhere ... until the Lord took him home. Did he urge you to write the book then, Gary?

After reading the manuscript that "says it all so clearly", I experienced delight and relief. Delight in the teaching – the clarity and humour – and relief that it is finally written down. I thought, "This is what the Vineyard is all about," as I read, over and over again, the stories about the Holy Spirit leading, us obeying and the wonders that occur in that partnership. I kept thinking, "I can do that! I can do that!" Well, even if I *have* done that, I was reminded that I can *still* do that – and do it more often!

In my opinion, this is a very important book. We in the Vineyard should all have a copy. No, two copies: One for yourself and one for a friend!

Thank you, thank you, thank you, Gary. I know John, in heaven, is delighted!

INTRODUCTION

In the spring of 1984, Blaine Cook came to our community church to do a conference on the kingdom of God. We had just become aware of a man named John Wimber, the founder of the Vineyard movement, who was teaching a course at Fuller Seminary called "Signs, Wonders and Church Growth", and had called to see if anyone would be available to introduce these concepts to us. Much to our surprise, John responded favourably to our call and sent Blaine, his close associate. My expectation for this conference was not particularly high. The kingdom of God was not a familiar term to me. I knew, of course, that it existed in the New Testament (the Lord's Prayer immediately came to mind), but beyond that, it had little significance for me.

Blaine's message on the first evening was a simple overview of the kingdom message that John had encountered through his involvement at Fuller. Blaine explained from Scripture how the kingdom or rule of God had broken into this present evil age through Jesus. He explained the signs and wonders associated with Jesus' ministry as characteristics of the next age breaking into the present as a result of Jesus' obedience to his Father. He went on to argue that we, the present-day disciples of Jesus, have been given this same ministry. "The Great Commission cannot simply be a call to proclamation," he said, echoing the heart of John Wimber's teaching. "It must include all the works that Jesus did – both his works of service and his works of power."

As I listened to this message, a strange thing was happening inside of me. It was as though I was playing a game of chess with God's Spirit. With every point of Blaine's talk, I could almost hear God's voice inside me saying, "Check!" (Given the standard at which I play chess, I am quite familiar with that term!) By the time Blaine demonstrated from John 14:12 that the kingdom call included *all* that Jesus did, "Checkmate" was ringing in my head and heart. I knew that I had just signed up for life as a messenger of the kingdom, bearing Good News in both words and deeds – including "signs and wonders".

I didn't have the slightest idea how that would ever be accomplished. No hint of the supernatural was evident in any part of my personality, or so I thought. The realm of the Spirit was very nebulous for me. While I had seen some seemingly otherworldly displays by people on stages (and suspected that at least some of it may have been genuine), I certainly never expected to see any of those kinds of things happen in my life. If God intended to do any of the works of power that Jesus did through me, he would certainly have a challenge on his hands!

At that time, I hadn't yet begun to understand the key insight that John gained from the kingdom message: Anyone could potentially do anything that Jesus did simply because kingdom power is rooted in obedience rather than being specially "anointed". Because John truly believed that the

Great Commission was in itself an empowered commission, he could teach with confidence that "everyone can play". If we would simply do what Jesus authorized us to do (proclaim the Good News and demonstrate it as the Holy Spirit directed us), we could rely on his power to effect his desired results.

The chapters that follow are my journey (and, of course, the journey of others with me) in severely testing this thesis. Often along the way, I would remark to myself, "If God can use me to do these things, he can certainly use anyone." My assessment after twenty years is emphatically: God can indeed use us all in the most unexpected ways. Repeatedly, over the past two decades, I have experienced the touch, in me and through me, of the divine, powerful hand of God – though I have rarely felt that my feet have left the ground. This book is dedicated to the conviction that this experience of being naturally supernatural is accessible to every follower of Jesus.

READING THE WORDS, DOING THE WORKS

INTRODUCTION TO THE STUDY GUIDE

Naturally Supernatural chronicles twenty years of walking out the call not just to hear the Word, but to put it into practice. James instructs us: "Do not merely listen to the word and so deceive yourselves, do what it says" (James 1:22). At the end of each chapter, you will find a section called Reading the Words, Doing the Works. This study guide will help you to chew over the material and digest it so that it can become part of your everyday life and practice. The study can be used by a small group or with a friend.

Since these questions are simply a tool to help you, feel free to choose whether to respond to all the questions or just the ones that seem most appropriate for you or your group. You may wish to add your own questions. Listen to the whispering of God in the questions you are most drawn to. Look for the specific areas he seems to be stirring in you.

FOR GROUP FACILITATORS

If you do this study as a group, it should take at least seven weeks, possibly longer. Week 1 should be an introduction by the facilitator, where group members are familiarized with the general content of the book, called to commit to the reading and respond to questions on their own each week and then paired up with another group member to pray for one another during the week as God begins to instruct them. In Week 2 members should come prepared to interact with the larger group, having read Chapter 1 and responded to the questions individually. It will be helpful for the facilitator to lead the group interactions.

Weeks 2–7 follow a similar format. Be sure to finish with a celebratory wrap-up!

JOINING GOD IN HIS WORK

JESUS' POWERFUL INVITATION

Of all the Gospel accounts in the New Testament, Mark's Gospel most emphasizes the immediacy of God's kingdom. Everything seems to happen, in his words, "at once", "quickly" or "immediately". In fact, it takes less than half of the first chapter for Jesus to be introduced and baptized by John, confronted head-on by Satan himself and to preach in Galilee in the power of the Spirit.

What was his message? Mark summarizes it succinctly in 1:15: "At last the time has come! The kingdom of God is near! Turn from your sins and believe this Good News." Setting aside for a moment the challenge of contextual distance (the fact that Jesus' first hearers would have understood much more easily what he meant by these words),[1] just how good was this Good News? Or, perhaps more personally, what do we expect of this news today?

---

[1] For a readable explanation of what Jesus meant in his original context, read N.T. Wright, *The Challenge of Jesus: Rediscovering Who Jesus Was and Is* (Downers Grove, IL: InterVarsity Press, 1999).

A few years ago, just before Christmas, I had a very unusual and unexpected encounter. I had been travelling extensively and, I'm sorry to say, had determined that I had certainly and sufficiently done my duty for the year and deserved to take the rest of the year off from active ministry. It was at this point that Joy, my wife, let me know that someone that I had known in my childhood had phoned earlier in the day in great distress. I remember thinking, "Well, I hope he is not in much greater distress in the new year, because he is not hearing from me. That is one phone call I'm not going to return."

Of course, as these things usually work out, right at that moment the phone rang and it was this man. (He had lived across the road from my family home for a few years, but was quite a bit younger than I. I remembered little of his story other than that his father was an alcoholic and quite abusive.) My first thought was that I could simply listen to his plight, pray for him or counsel him on the phone and/or hopefully refer him to someone who would be best qualified to help him further. Joy felt quite differently. She had been praying at that very time for an increase in our experience of healing and deliverance. As I answered the phone, she mouthed the words, "It's the Lord!" She was convinced that this call was an answer to her prayers.

I was little prepared emotionally or spiritually for the plight that I encountered. To shorten a long and tragic story, soon after his father had left the home (I had moved away as well), this young boy was deceived by a man who befriended him and eventually coerced into an international drug smuggling ring where he was used as a courier and sex slave under threat of death (his own and his family's). This continued until his mid-teens, when he confided in an uncle who was a member of a biker gang. His uncle simply said, "I'll take care of it." Whatever this relative did obviously made a difference. For some months there was no contact from those who had previously tormented him. Upon hearing, however, of the mysterious death of his uncle, the now teenaged boy fled to another city. Within a year or so, he had literally lost all memory of his enslaved childhood. His inner life had shut down completely.

In some ways, he was then able to lead a "normal" life – he married, raised two children and was able to hold down a regular job. Under the surface of conscious memory, however, the fear and trauma continually undermined his best efforts. He struggled with many addictions and would be driven to occasional binges, when these internal forces overwhelmed him. Finally, at age forty-two, just a few days before he called me, all his coping mechanisms collapsed. It started with a flashback that quickly resulted in his entire childhood memory flooding in. He collapsed in a full seizure and was taken to the psychiatric unit of the local hospital. For some days, his body was racked with physical pain, his mind terrorized by fear.

As I reluctantly listened to this story, I must confess that I thought to myself, "I am too exhausted even to want to deal with this. And even if I weren't, this situation is too overwhelming and complex." His attitude wasn't helping to convince me otherwise. He seemed quite embittered towards God. In fact, he went out of his way to emphasize to me that he preferred the term "Great Power" and didn't even want me using "God". I remember thinking, "Buddy, if you don't even want to use the word 'God', go get a shrink or somebody – it's all I've got!"

Of course, my pastoral training has taught me to with-hold what I am really thinking. Instead, I offered to pray for him. In retrospect, I realize my offer was not coming from the best of motives. If I must be honest, my prayer was a way of closing the conversation. I didn't really expect anything to happen. I just prayed a little prayer. Have you every tried to pray a prayer without using "God" in it? After awhile, just to spite him, I used the word "God" anyway. It was much like this: "Oh God, give him peace and help the pain to go away and open a way for him." That was it.

You can imagine my surprise when he called the next day to report, somewhat excitedly, that the pain had largely disappeared. My inner response was, "You must be kidding. Man, if that kind of prayer can work, anything can work." From that first encouragement, his heart began to soften and my heart had a small measure of hope that God might actually be at work in this situation. After some more "telephone prayer", we arranged to visit him just after Christmas. In that encounter, we had an opportunity to pray for him once more – this time in person. Using the word "God" was no longer a problem.

His situation still seemed overwhelming. He was liter-ally terrorized by demonic oppression and fear and as a result didn't even have the courage to go out in public. Not knowing entirely where to begin, I asked (because of the history of abuse) if he would be willing to see a friend of mine who worked with an international ministry called Living Waters that helps people with sexual and relational prob-lems. The challenge was that it was an hour's drive each way. Surprisingly, he had the faith and courage to believe that he could venture out from the safety of his home for that long.

As I picked him up on the appointed day, I considered how best to use the two hours that I would have with him on the drive. As I thought about it, I realized that God was certainly his only hope. At the same time, he had no idea who God really was. Jim (not his real name) primarily envisioned God as an angry old man in the sky who was frustrated because he had too many children. He just wanted to slap them around every once in a while because they wouldn't behave. Jim was quite sure that the only way you could get onto this God's good side would be by being really good – something at which he, quite frankly, had never been very successful. As a result, God was someone he tried to avoid or, at least, to ignore.

As we began our drive, I said, "Jim, I'd like to tell you the story of God's Book, the Bible. You think you know what this Book has to say, but I don't think you understand it at all. You actually don't know this is good news. You think it's bad news. You are wondering why anybody printed it. Isn't that right?"

For the next hour, starting at the beginning of Genesis, I began to tell him the amazing story of God's grace. For the entire trip into the city, I told him the story of the Old Testament. "The story of the Old Testament is not difficult to identify with," I said. "It is filled with people just like you and me. We see humanity just as it really is – at times at its very worst. Yet the amazing part of the story is God's response: He simply won't give up on us. He just keeps loving us! Grace upon grace."

As I went on telling this story of God's heart for his creation, Jim kept looking at me incredulously. "Are you sure this is true?" he asked.

"Yes," I said, "it really is."

"Nobody I know knows this," he replied. He was implying: "If you guys are trying to keep this a secret, you're doing a really good job. Because everybody thinks you're saying something completely different. Nobody knows this!"

After his appointment, on our way home, we launched into the second half of the story. "Now, Jim," I said, "here's where it gets really good. Because now, Jesus, the answer to which all of this first part of the Book points, is introduced."

I began to explain Mark 1, where Jesus says: "The time has come, now the answer to the deepest longings of your heart and the longing of God's heart has come near you, is within your reach." I explained the amazing offer of God through Jesus – one not based on performance or sacrifice, but an invitation completely initiated by the mercy of God alone. As we pulled up to his driveway, I said, "Jesus is coming near you, Jim."

As I stopped the car, there was a pause. Jim looked at me and finally said, "Well, what do I do?"

"This is different," I said. "This is big. This isn't like just smoking a joint and somehow you get a Jesus experience. No, this is actually a trade: You give him your whole life (which, I added, the last time I checked was not that great) and you get his, but you absolutely have to surrender to him. Sorry, there is no cheaper buy-in than that."

He looked at me and replied, "Let's do this thing." So we went in and started to pray.

"Jim," I said, "this is kind of what you do. You just start offering yourself to God. You don't need any special religious vocabulary. Just speak out of your heart as though you were speaking to me. As you do, God's Spirit will start to show you specific things that you need to give to him. Just obey his promptings."

This is what he did for perhaps a quarter to half an hour. While he was praying these things, I was repeating silently John Wimber's classic Vineyard prayer, "Oh God, oh God this is going to take a miracle." Then, after a while, Jim stopped, looked at me and said, "This isn't working."

This is everyone's worst-case "evangelistic nightmare" scenario! What do you say next? "Well, Jim," I said, "you know what? You took several years getting into this mess. It might take more than half an hour to get out of it. Maybe God is busy or something – just redial. He cares very much about the cries of your heart. Begin to talk to God as though he were the Dad that you always wished you had."

Somewhat reluctantly, he began to pray again. Shortly thereafter, he dropped suddenly to his knees. "Thank you, Jesus," I thought. "Now he is getting serious." Next he dropped to his face. "Ouch," I said to myself. Then he began to shake all over. "This could be God," I remarked. Then he started to bounce on the floor and I thought, "Oh my!" This went on for some time. I didn't really know what to do. I just kept asking God to take control of his life while practising the laying on and the laying off of hands as he bounced (On … Off … On … Off …). This continued with incredible intensity for some time until he suddenly cried out between clenched teeth, "Call 911!"

"I don't think so, Jim," I replied. "I think this is actually better than it feels." I began to pray that God's Spirit would drive out all demonic power, fill and cleanse him with the Holy Spirit. Finally, after a significant period of time, it was as though someone just pulled a plug and everything became absolutely still. I detected a pulse. "That's encouraging," I thought. "At least he's alive." I said, "Jim, are you all right?" He sat up a little and just stared into space, not speaking.

I tried to explain that I was flying out the next day for a short trip and needed to leave but that I really believed he was going to be all right, that I thought God had really done something significant. I left him a Bible and I showed him some helpful places to read. He still hardly said anything – he just had a glazed look in his eye. As I walked out of the door, I remember thinking, "I sure hope that was all right!"

Two days later, as I walked into the office, my coworker met me with the remark, "I don't know who this guy is, but he has been calling all morning."

"Oh no," I thought. "He's going to sue. Something must have gone wrong. Maybe he broke his nose or something."

"You didn't tell me it was this good!" were the first words that boomed from the phone.

"What do you mean?" I asked.

He began to explain what happened to him once he began crying out to God from the depths of his heart: God started a dialogue with him, asking him to trust him and to surrender different parts of his life to him. At one point, God asked him if Jim could trust enough to forgive those who had abused him. "My answer initially was no," Jim said, "until finally I was able to say, 'In Jesus' name, I forgive them.' When those words were expressed from my heart, it was as though my body was plugged into an electric circuit!"

Jim explained what he was experiencing while he was shaking on the floor. First there was a burning sensation, like fire that started in his feet. As he continued shaking and trembling, this fire began to move up through his body. As it did so, he could feel different physical conditions being completely healed and righted as it touched them. (The symptoms of five different ailments, some quite serious, disappeared immediately and, to this day, have never returned.) When the fire reached his throat, which was chronically irritated due to years of constant smoking, it was completely restored and he thought, "Great, now I can smoke dope with no pain!"

By the time this power reached the top of his head, he felt like a totally new, free person. His eyes were opened and he could see demonic powers. In fact, after I left, he was swinging a towel at them in his bedroom yelling, "Get out of here." When his wife got home and found him, she was ready to call 911. In fact, she was still a little traumatized a week later, thinking, "Who is this guy?"

Jim's whole life began to be transformed from the inside out. His previous addictions no longer had any hold on him. He began attending a church near where he lived. Soon the rest of his family came to Jesus as well. When I recently talked with him, he was coordinating a significant, ongoing outreach to children from poor areas at his church. He is witnessing to the Good News about Jesus everywhere he goes. In the beginning, he was an evangelist to Christians. Whenever he would encounter one, he would challenge them: "Why are you keeping this a secret? This is the best news anyone could ever hear – you must share it!"

HOW GOOD IS THE GOOD NEWS?

Why did I take so long to tell that story? The question I asked was this: "How good is the Good News?" One of the great

tragedies of modern Christianity is that we have expected far
too little of eternal life. Perhaps the best-known Scripture in
the entire Bible is John 3:16: "For God so loved the world
that he gave his only Son that everyone who believes in
him will not perish but have eternal life." Yet many, myself
included, have somehow mistakenly understood that eternal
life is something that happens at the end of our earthly lives.
As a result, we have put all our energy into trying to get people into heaven instead of trying to get heaven into people.
We have tried to get people, as the American author Dallas
Willard says, ready to die rather than getting them ready to
live.[2] No wonder we haven't been very good advertising for
God. Jesus' explanation of eternal life was very different: He
offered life in all its fullness now, life to the fullest extent in
every part of who we are (John 10:10), that begins when we
first come to Jesus and simply continues toward even greater
vitality throughout eternity. That is the Good News! That is
what Jesus is offering when he proclaims "the kingdom of
God is near" (Mark 1:15).

The ensuing chapters of Mark's Gospel clearly illustrate the nature and intent of Jesus' invitation: God's rule
released through Jesus reaches into the oppressed state of
people's lives and dramatically brings life and freedom. We
see Jesus casting out an evil spirit (vs. 21–28) – in the synagogue of all places! Quickly the news began to spread. "This
is what Jesus means by 'Good News'." Most likely, reports
were also shared in the community about Jesus' healing of
Simon's mother-in-law and by sunset (once the Sabbath was
over), the whole village brought their sick and demonically

---

[2]Dallas Willard, *Renovation of the Heart: Putting on the Character
of Christ* (Colorado Springs: NavPress, 2002), pages 238–239.

oppressed to Jesus. Mark tells us that a huge crowd gathered outside to watch as Jesus healed great numbers of those who came to him. The next morning, people were lined up saying, "This is Good News!"

Next in Mark's account, Jesus encounters a leprous man, one of the untouchables in ancient Near Eastern society. Yet Jesus, moved with compassion, touched him and embraced him, restoring him completely. Further shock waves ran through the whole community – how much better could this get? This continues throughout the Gospel of Mark and all the Gospels: This is what Jesus came to do.

In his hometown of Nazareth, Jesus responded to the implicit question: "What is it that you are about?" He made it clear that he had come in fulfilment of the messianic prophecy of Isaiah 61:1: "The Spirit of God has anointed me and set me apart. He has empowered me to give life and freedom to the brokenness and the oppression that Satan's kingdom has inflicted on God's created ones."

This is all-encompassing Good News! It touches the tangible needs of the poor. It touches the physical tragedies that affect their lives. It touches those who are crushed by all sorts of oppression. It sets the prisoners free. This Good News touches every aspect of their lives!

The Kingdom of God Is Near

But what of us today? Perhaps John Wimber's greatest contribution was his insistence that the Good News then is the Good News now. John recognized that Jesus' invitation to us today is still the same: To enjoy eternal life in all its fullness – beginning now and continuing eternally. Of course, John was clear, as are the Scriptures, that we don't and won't have heaven yet. We are never going to break what theologians call eschatological tension. In this life, there will always be the already/not yet – the co-existence of this present evil age alongside the in-breaking age to come.

There will therefore always be an aspect of incompleteness in this present life. There will also be an active resistance to this Good News by the powers of this age (which control our culture). They want to bring you back "in line" and prevent others from hearing the Good News and submitting to Jesus. Nevertheless, we can expect a taste of all of the powers of heaven to come to us in one way or another, in every aspect of our lives. Far beyond simply "going to heaven" one day, the Good News tells us to expect, in some measure, the full benefits of heaven beginning to come to us here and now.

In order to understand this, let's take a closer look at Jesus' announcement in Mark 1:15. At the beginning of our discussion, I pointed out that the people in Jesus' day, simply because of their first-century Jewish background, would have had a much clearer understanding of the Old Testament context of the term "kingdom" than we would generally have today.[3] What few kingdoms remain are (1) ruled by a monarch without significant power, and (2) confused with geographic locations as a result of their being identified with the nation-states of the modern era.

Dallas Willard has written several brilliant books that

---

[3]My very brief and somewhat simple examination of the kingdom of God certainly doesn't do justice to the subject. The reader would benefit greatly from reading Derek Morphew's *Breakthrough: Discovering the Kingdom* (Cape Town: Vineyard International Publishing, 2001). Derek's book, though written by a theologian, is accessible to the reader and brings this theology within reach.

are very timely for the church, at least in the Western world. In *The Divine Conspiracy*, he defines this term "kingdom" as the "range of one's effective will".[4] What does this mean? It means the extent to which our "wishing" or "willing" is actually realized. In the course of my life, I have wished I could do many things. As a young father, I wished that my children would always obey me cheerfully. As a leader, I have wished that my life could be lived without any conflict. A wish and reality are two different things.

Your real kingdom is measured by the degree to which what you want done actually is done. In Matthew 6, Jesus instructed his disciples to pray: "Your kingdom come, your will be done." Where God's will is done, his kingdom is present. Where our will is done, our kingdom is present. Actually, this expression of our will is an essential part of being made in the image of God, of being a person.[5] Without any opportunity to see our will accomplished, our personhood cannot be developed or expressed. We need to be the boss of something.

Who is God the boss of? How big is his kingdom?

---

[4] Dallas Willard, *The Divine Conspiracy: Rediscovering Our Hidden Life in God* (San Francisco: HarperSanFrancisco, 1998), pages 21–22.

[5] This is not to say that physically challenged persons who cannot "will" their bodies to function in a certain way are not real persons. Rather, the point is simply that God's perfect intention is that all his created ones could fully express the unique characteristics of his image within them; factors that limit this expression are enemies of God's desire for us. Of course, God can and does use this suffering for a redemptive purpose in our lives. Many people with physical disabilities rise above these challenges to express powerfully the unique personhood that is God's gift to them. (Stephen Hawking comes to mind.)

When we read the very beginning of the Bible and are introduced to the beginning of the world, God is already there. God was before all things; he precedes all of his creation. He made all there is. In Colossians 1:17, Paul reminds us that he not only made all things, but that additionally "he [Christ] holds all creation together". Everything is in God's kingdom!

Our History in the Kingdom

We discover when we read the first two chapters of Genesis that, in making us in his image, it was always God's intention to give us a kingdom. God not only created the first man and woman; he also gave them a stewardship, a "kingdom". He said: "Be masters over the earth and all these created things on the earth; rule over the birds of the air, the fish of the sea and the animals. Master this world and steward it, and in full cooperation with me, continue to nurture and enhance the beauty of this created place."

As we read on in Scripture, we realize that this was just the beginning. From before the foundation of the world, God's plan was for us to reign with him in his eternal kingdom – our stewardship of the world is a training ground of sorts. His purpose is that we exercise our will fully in complete harmony with his and together do something magnificent for this world. As we know, that plan was short-circuited; by the third chapter of Genesis, something devastating had happened.

We are seduced and we rebel – we try to set up our "kingdom" independently of God, to be the judges of the earth, pushing God off his "throne". Consequently, far from gaining our autonomy, we are separated from the wonderful protection of God's kingdom and are drawn into bondage in another kingdom, one of darkness. It is the kingdom of Satan, God's enemy. All of creation is cursed by this oppressive rule. Something has gone desperately wrong; the harmony and peace of the garden has been shattered. As we continue to read the ensuing chapters of Genesis, the narrative has the sound and feeling of a plane plummeting out of the sky, about to crash.

Without the benefit of hindsight, we would probably expect God simply to pull the plug – yet surprisingly, he doesn't. As we continue to read through the Old Testament, we realize that he fully intends to fulfil what he promised almost immediately after the fall and separation of humankind (Genesis 3:15): God will raise up a descendant of the woman who will bring about the deliverance of his created ones from Satan's domination.

These promises continue through the darkest valleys of the subsequent history of God's chosen ones. Again and again, through various prophets, God reassures: "I haven't given up on you. I will fulfil my promise. There is going to be deliverance." "At just the right time," he says, "I will respond to you. On the day of salvation I will help you" (Isaiah 49:8). Through Isaiah, Jeremiah and Ezekiel – but also through many other prophetic times, places and messengers – God reinforces the same message: "At the right time, I will come and rescue you. I will bring you out of this kingdom of darkness into my glorious kingdom again." This longing, expectation and hope runs through the Old Testament.

Then, at just the right time, writes Paul in Galatians 4:4, Jesus explodes onto the scene. Quite apart from any worthy accomplishment that might have compelled God to act, God's mercy alone determines that this is the time. In fact, hope and expectation are at a very low ebb. The Son of Man comes and finds very little faith on the earth. When he is least expected, the deliverer comes to bring us out of captivity in Satan's dark kingdom and release us into life and freedom (Colossians 1:13–14).

The Humility of Grace

When we read this story, we cannot help but recognize that God seems to do just about all of it. That is the amazing thing that so shocks people when they actually read the Bible. There is no place for religion, if by "religion" we mean earning a place of merit before God. He does it all. All … except one thing, according to Jesus' Good News. There is something that we need to do. It is repeatedly made clear in the invitation of Jesus. In the compilation of Jesus' core teaching, known as the Sermon on the Mount (Matthew 5–7), Jesus points out the central factor that determines whether or not God's free gift of grace is successful in touching our lives: "God blesses those who realize their need for him" (Matthew 5:3).

It is only when we recognize our great poverty, humble ourselves and cry out for mercy, that we can receive the free gift of life through Jesus. The one thing we can do – must do – is to turn from our self-reliance and reach for the Good News. We do just the opposite of what happened in Eden. Instead of trying to be independent of God, we surrender and submit to his rule. We do not do anything to obtain the Good News; we just submit to it. It is always near to us, but we must reach for it … again and again. The Gospels are filled with accounts of those who did just that.

Often when I am speaking about this offer of grace, I try to illustrate tangibly the necessity of responding humbly but actively in order to receive it. I pray and ask God to show me an amount of money that I personally should offer the audience that has come to hear me teach. At times the amount that I feel I am to give is quite significant. (In one Asian country, it was about one month's wage for the average worker.) I then hold out the money and offer it to anyone who needs it. Invariably, at first no one moves – they think it is just an illustration, that I am not really serious about the offer.

Usually I have to ask the questions: "Has this offer benefited anyone yet? When will this actually help anyone?" Amazingly, even when it becomes clear that my offer is a serious one, many are still hesitant, though they know that they have real need. What holds them back? A variety of factors: Sometimes embarrassment (perhaps they aren't dressed appropriately); sometimes a sense of unworthiness (someone else might need the gift more than they do), sometimes pride (they didn't do anything to deserve this gift). Once one person musters the courage to stride forward and take it, the impact is felt by all – the gift could have been theirs! The lesson is clear: The ones who receive the gift are the ones who simply reach for and take it. The Gospels are filled with accounts of those who did just that.

We must believe that the offer is real, we must realize our need for it and we must reach out to take it. The truth is that the mercy of God is absolutely free and inexhaustible: As long as there is a desire to stretch out our hand, the kingdom of God is near enough to reach. That is the message of this Good News. We do not have to wait until we can make some great spiritual sacrifice that will close the gap between God and ourselves. We simply have to acknowledge that we need God's grace and turn toward it, just as we are.

RELEASING THE GOOD NEWS

John Wimber's second main contribution was to remind the evangelical church of the full biblical implication of the Great Commission. To "go and make disciples" (Matthew 28:19) means to partner with God and have the authority to release this wonderful taste of life from the coming age to others who will receive it. In other words, God has entrusted the ministry of Jesus to us. Just as God anointed Jesus to announce and demonstrate the nearness of God's kingdom, he has authorized us to do the same today. It seems difficult to believe that God would make this decision – after all, he made us and knows us, along with our dismal track record. Nevertheless, he confidently intends to restore us to a place of coworking with him, both in this age and in the age to come.

The First Disciples

We see this plan at work in those who first respond to Jesus' message and began to follow him. As they received and believed the Good News, submitting to the authority of Jesus, the love and presence of God began to capture their hearts and transform them from the inside out. Their conscious desire was increasingly to become just like Jesus, both who he was and what he did. More and more, they cared about the things that God cares about, that Jesus modelled for them. They were experiencing eternal life, the kingdom of God established and establishing within them. Over time we see this kingdom life not only filling and changing them, but also creating a growing desire to see this life and freedom come to others.

This, of course, was Jesus' intention from the very beginning when he first called them. "Follow me," he said, but his ultimate purpose was that God would use them to be and bring Good News to others as well (Mark 1:17; 3:13–15). His intention was that they would do the very things he did – even his works of power.

At first the disciples did everything with Jesus, which I'm sure was a great delight for them – Jesus' ministry times always worked! I can imagine working alongside Jesus, laying hands on sick people. Certainly it would be a wonderful experience. No doubt the prayer would be successful every time. But after a while, I would want to take my hand off just for a moment and then put it back again. Why? I would want to see if it made any difference. My thinking would be: "It always works when Jesus does it, but am I making any difference?"

Were the first disciples at all like me? It wouldn't surprise me. The New Testament clearly portrays them as very human. Of course, they at least knew that their efforts couldn't mess it up. When they prayed along with Jesus, it worked. But what if Jesus wasn't there? That possibility was tested soon enough: Jesus gathered the Twelve to commission them for just such an adventure. "We are going to do a little ministry trip," he told them. "It will be just like the others with one slight exception: You are going to do it without me" (Matthew 10:1–10). No doubt this brought a major question into the minds of the disciples: Would Jesus' commissioning be enough? Could they actually do the things that they had seen Jesus do on the basis of his authority alone?

All that Luke tells us (9:10) about this first ministry excursion is that they did it – the implication is that they had some success. I suspect, however, that it was not without some trepidation on their part because, even after a second commissioned tour (this one involving approximately sixty others), their response on their return gives them away – you know how anxious they were by how excited they are when they get back! The essence of their enthusiastic response, recorded in Luke 10, is basically this: "It even works if you send us; it works without you even being there! Even the demons flee from us as they did from you!" Of course, this was Jesus' plan all along; it was always his intention to leave them doing all that he had begun.

There is something very significant about this second ministry trip. It tells us that the special ability to do the same works of power that Jesus was demonstrating is not just reserved for the anointed Twelve, the "men of power for the hour". Seemingly anyone who Jesus commissions can do the same.

Jesus' ultimate intention, however, was never to restrict this commission to just a few – twelve or seventy-two. We begin to discover that his goal all along has been to release an ever-increasing number of disciples, who are both sent and fully empowered to continue his ministry. In some of Jesus' last dialogues with the Twelve, he emphasizes this point (John 14). The disciples are understandably apprehensive about Jesus' intended departure. This absence is much more serious than their previous brief forays without him. Jesus' response to Philip is noteworthy: "Don't you understand?" he asks. "Anyone (not just the Twelve or the seventy-two), yes, anyone who believes in me will do all of the things that I have been doing – works of kindness, works of love, service, power, all of it." (John 14:9f) These things are simply what the apprentices of Jesus do.

This purpose is formalized during Jesus' post-resurrection interactions with the Twelve and others. Having risen from the grave, he holds the keys to death and hell with complete authority in heaven and on earth. There is no question that whatever commission he gives to his disciples will have the full backing of God's sovereign power. What is it that he authorizes them to do? "Go and make disciples of all nations." (Matthew 28:18–20)

Let's understand this clearly – the disciples don't receive this commission with a bewildered look on their faces, wondering what he could possibly be talking about. "What on earth is a disciple? How do you make a disciple?" These men had spent the last three years with Jesus intentionally modelling this process for them. They were not idiots; they knew he was saying: "What I did with you, do with others. Give it away so that there are a whole lot more who are doing all the things that I did, saying all the things I said and living according to the example I set." Finally, he adds: "And don't forget to teach these ones to do the same with still others."

Kingdom Disciples Today

What are the implications of this commission? From then to the present day, the history of Christianity should be characterized by intentional disciples of Jesus doing just what Jesus did, then passing it on to others. It is at the very least the primary meaning of being a follower of Jesus.

Somehow we have invented a Christianity that isn't that, a Christianity that is dangerously like "salt that has lost its savour" (Matthew 5:13). Functionally, we have too often kept the kingdom of God rather far away from our real lives, our faith trapped in a world of "private belief". The full potential of kingdom life does not come to us or flow freely through us.

The Good News of Jesus, however, is still the same. The kingdom of God is within our reach. If we will simply turn, acknowledge our need and reach for it, God's eternal life will come alive in and through us again.

THE KEY TO KINGDOM MINISTRY

All this Good News can be simultaneously deeply encouraging and somewhat intimidating – particularly God's intention to have the Good News released through us. When we realize that the commission to the first disciples (and, through them, to us) includes doing all that Jesus did (even his works of power), we can easily become overwhelmed by the task. It is challenging enough to embrace fully Jesus' works of love and service; accepting his command to his first disciples to "heal the sick, raise the dead, cure those with leprosy, and cast out demons" (Matthew 10:8) requires a whole new level of faith.

This can become a weight of expectation that grows in our minds until we feel we are supposed to raise the dead before breakfast. The only dead person I see raised before breakfast is me – and then only partially! It is exciting to have been given the ministry of Jesus, but we are definitely not Jesus. I often feel so unlike Jesus and so unable to follow his example that I fear my prayers may do more harm than good.

In British Columbia, learner drivers are required to place a large letter N in the rear window of the vehicle they are attempting to drive. It stands for "Novice Driver". It's a way of saying to other, more experienced drivers, "I'm just learning; you may want to drive on a different road." Often we feel we should have a similar sign placed on us as a warning when we run into people in the name of Jesus: "Be careful, I'm a new pray-er; I'm just learning."

We have been commissioned to continue the ministry of Jesus – all of it – in spite of our relative incompetence and limited faith. In this we are no different to the first disciples. Like them, we need to begin at the beginning and embrace the humbling process of being a learner. Where, then, should we begin? Is there a fundamental first principle around which we can centre our efforts? Is there a key understanding that will make this possible? Thankfully, there is. In John 5:1–20, Jesus reveals the guiding principle of how he himself, as a man, did his Father's works. This key that he passed on to his first disciples enabled them to walk in his power and authority.

The Key to Jesus' Works

Whenever Jesus spoke or acted, he did so with great authority – that much was recognized by all (Mark 1:22; 6:2), including the Pharisees who, while they vehemently opposed him, certainly didn't dismiss him. His teaching went far beyond the polished oratory of the religious leaders. It displayed a depth and weight that made the listener feel as though God himself were speaking. The common question was: "Where did this Galilean get such authority? He hasn't even apprenticed with a recognized religious teacher." John the Baptist's reply was simply: "He speaks God's words." (John 3:34) This was Jesus' own answer in response to that question. He would say: "Actually, I will tell you a little secret about my messages. I don't write them – God does!" (John 12:49–50)

I know that many pastors say the same thing (which has brought God's credibility as a writer into disrepute). But with Jesus, it was true: God the Father wrote his messages and Jesus repeated them. In fact, that applied to all his actions, as he explains in John 5. The context of his explanation was one of his regular conflicts with the religious leaders, who were constantly harassing him and trying to shut down his ministry. In this case, they were after him for breaking the Sabbath rules that they had defined rigorously. Jesus' response to them is very significant: "My Father never stops working, so why should I?" (John 5:17) This understanding was the absolute key to everything he did and the way he did it.

It is extremely important for us to understand this – all of us who have said "Yes" to the kingdom commission. It is very easy to fall into the trap of thinking that the Great Commission is something that we have to strap onto our backs and do *for* God. We expect to function like a spiritual machine, God's "great anointed ones," moving from miracle to miracle. This expectation comes from the false understanding that we are required to bring the kingdom of God single-handedly into the dark, difficult and unbelieving world around us. This theory says that once we have done the groundwork, God will add his part to finish things off – or at least join us in celebrating the victory, if we have already been successful.

Perhaps this kind of disciple really exists – constantly flowing in unrelenting spiritual power. If so, they seem to be largely confined to stages. I've met few in real life. Most are somewhat like me; they find it hard to save, heal, deliver and raise people from the dead with their own resident spiritual power – particularly when they themselves have a cold.

Jesus understood what we constantly forget: God never stops working. He is building and bringing his kingdom with and/or without us. While we sleep, he is actively establishing and extending his rule. Even while we are reading this information, God is working in us and all around us. His plan in inviting us to share in Jesus' work was never to leave us on our own (Matthew 28:20). His desire is to give us the privilege of joining him in his work.

Jesus understood perfectly his limitations as a created human being. He said, "I assure you, the Son can do nothing by himself" (John 5:19). He was the Son of God, but since he was also fully human, he understood that he could not act independently. He could only do what his Father authorized him to do. This is what he did: When he heard what God wanted to do or saw him at work, he simply put his hand to God's. He only did what he saw his Father doing. This was the key to his great authority: Because he and his Father always acted in complete unity, Jesus' visible part of the partnership had the full strength of heaven behind it.

Naturally, it helped to be the sinless Son of God. There was no interference from sinful habits to distort his hearing. There was no impediment to absolute trust in his Father. The Holy Spirit completely filled him. As a result, he always did what pleased the Father and only spoke what the Father desired (John 8:29; 12:50).

Following Jesus' Example

It is a little more of a challenge for us because we don't hear as completely as Jesus and we don't trust the Father as Jesus did. As a result, our obedience is often misdirected or half-hearted. Yet, even if imperfectly, we can do what Jesus did. If we begin to realize that God is at work all around us, and that he has prepared a part in that work for us, our whole task is different. It is simply a matter of finding God and putting our hand to his. It is just seeing what God is doing and understanding what he is authorizing us to join him. Whatever it is that God has prepared as our part – whether something visibly powerful like healing, deliverance or miracles or something less visible like works of kindness, generosity or love – if we join him in it, the full grace of heaven can be released.

Some years ago, Joy and I attended a conference hosted by a group of Canada's First Nations believers. The purpose of the conference was to explore the issue of contextualization of the gospel within aboriginal culture, i.e. to what degree some of the cultural forms of Canada's first people could be utilized in their worship of Jesus. I was invited to speak at the first session to provide an overall framework for the weekend.

Being sensitive to honour our First Nations traditions, the conference hosts had invited the Grand Chief of the territory where the conference was held to welcome the participants officially and bring his greetings. He was a well-spoken, kind and gracious man, a lawyer by profession. As he gave his welcome address, he was in obvious pain – he shared that he had injured his back playing basketball with his son and had almost decided not to come. It was clear to see that he fulfilled his duties with great discomfort.

After his greeting, there was a short break before I was scheduled to speak. Joy and I took the opportunity to thank him for being so gracious to welcome us even though he understandably would have some tension with our beliefs. In the middle of our brief conversation, it became clear to Joy that there was a greater agenda than expressing our appreciation. It was not a coincidence that he had suffered this injury. Perhaps God wanted to heal him. Without hesitating to assess the risks that such an announcement might bring, she simply asked him if he would be willing to let us pray for his back. Amazingly he said, "Yes."

Almost immediately, as we began to pray (asking Jesus to release his healing power into this man's back), his back began to twitch, then jerk. Soon he began to shake as the power of God's Spirit came upon him. He was very aware of the power that was touching his body as we prayed in the name of Jesus. Within a few short minutes, his back was completely free of pain through its entire range of motion. Tears of gratitude filled his eyes. Something had touched his heart deeply. The presence of God's Spirit had awakened the image of God in him and was drawing him.

After the break, he again took the stage to tell the crowd what had happened to him. He then took a drum and, while playing it, began to sing a spontaneous song. I remember some of the words: "Oh Great Spirit, I give my life to you in love and devotion ..." He took a significant step in his spiritual journey toward the Father of all that day because Joy dared to put her hand to what she believed the Father wanted to do.

Understanding this principle of joining God in his work changes everything. All around us – where we work, play, live – is an absolute setup. God has uniquely placed us in the centre of his kingdom activity and he has specially gifted us to be and to express Good News to those in whom he has already been working. Our only task is to open our eyes and ears to begin to see the signs of his presence and to touch all around us. This is not to say that doing so is a simple undertaking.

When I was first being trained in this, I was often instructed during "practice sessions" to observe what was happening with people as God was touching them. "The Holy Spirit is touching this person. Can you see what he is doing?" they would say. I would walk around to the back, then to the front and still I couldn't see the Holy Spirit for the life of me. Once, at the end of the evening, somebody said, "What do you think?" In my frustration, I remarked, "I feel like a blind man at a film festival. There are all sorts of things happening here and I can't see any of it."

Similarly, it sometimes takes considerable faith to believe that God is actually at work around us each day at home, at school or in our workplace. Most often the drawing work of God's Spirit is invisible to the undiscerning eye. (In fact, Satan works overtime to immobilize us by trying to convince us that God's kingdom is far away from our regular spheres of activity, beyond our reach.) The Gospels show clearly how Jesus' first followers initially struggled to grow in this discernment, yet it is encouraging to see how they grew over time. I too have found that God's kingdom is near enough so that even a blind man like me can begin to see its presence and enter in.

READING THE WORDS,
DOING THE WORKS

DISCUSS IT

Gary talks about "seeing what God is doing" and "joining him in his work".

- How do you respond to this concept?
- Is this something you are comfortable with and practice or something that you would like to learn?
- Did God bring someone across your path this past week who may have presented you with an opportunity to do just that? Share the experience and how you responded.

If you did not respond in the way you think God may have been asking:

- What held you back? The Holy Spirit always guides his people. He will already be guiding you in areas where you need to grow.
- Are there fears you need to dare to face?
- Is there sin you need to repent of?
- Share them with your partner. Pray about it together.

Share a time when you did respond to God's direction.

Why is the Good News good to you? Share specifically.

DO IT
- Ask the Lord to give you an opportunity this week to practise what you have been learning.
- Whether you are just growing in this or are seasoned in it, it may be helpful to have a buddy join you when you offer to pray for someone.

PRAY ABOUT IT
Lord, I give you my next week. I ask you to guide my steps. I will keep my eyes open to see what you are doing. I ask for strength to respond with boldness, offering to pray for whatever situation you bring across my path. I give my brothers and sisters the right to hold me accountable next week. I will try to enjoy this adventure, not just enduring or resenting it. Amen, let your kingdom come!

THINK ABOUT IT
To develop a listening ear to God's voice, you will need time in God's Word, time alone focused on listening to his voice and time to pour out the desire of your heart to him. Don't be afraid to ask for big answers for your desires to learn his kingdom ways. Let him teach you over the course of the rest of your life!

CHAPTER 2

GOD'S POWERFUL TOOLS

NATURALLY SUPERNATURAL

We are natural people who have been invited and called to an amazing supernatural task.[1] We have the keys to the kingdom. We get to unlock doors that can't be unlocked in any other than a supernatural way and welcome people into the most incredible "eternal life" transformation that begins now and continues forever.

If we are simply willing to try to see what God is doing and take the risk of reaching out to put our hands with his, anything can happen. A miracle is potentially within our reach at any moment. It doesn't matter how we feel. It doesn't matter how well or poorly we speak. It doesn't matter how brilliantly we perform. If we happen to catch hold

---

[1]The terms "supernatural" and "miraculous" (though "miracles" are certainly referenced in Scripture) make many theologians nervous as they seem to imply that God is distant or not involved most of the time – that he only breaks into history once in a while to do something that is not "natural" (thus supernatural) or to perform a miracle. Another way of looking at his action is that he is always involved in history, but that we only notice his action once in a while, when he does something that looks unusual to us.

of what God is desiring to do, all heaven can break loose.

Our first Vineyard church plant in Canada, in 1985, was an amazing experience. Seemingly in spite of our best efforts, it grew dramatically. While this brought many benefits, one of the drawbacks was that, after six or seven years, most leadership opportunities were being filled by "older and wiser" leaders (for us that meant people in their thirties). This concerned me greatly. I believe strongly that one of the best ways to learn and grow is to get out there and try new things. (This reminds me of the scene in the movie *Shrek* where the donkey is jumping up and down around the circle saying, "Pick me, pick me!") There was only one solution: Create a new opportunity in which to learn and lead that was exclusively reserved for those in their teens and twenties.

We created a Friday night service or congregation of the church called God Rock that no one over thirty could go to except my wife and I. (There was no way we were going to miss out on the fun!) We took a deliberately hard-core approach. We intentionally scheduled it on a Friday night – supposedly a night when few young people would come. We started at about 7 p.m. for prayer, and sometimes we would continue until 1 a.m. We would have two or three ministry times every night. The house rules went like this: If you weren't a follower of Jesus, you weren't required to pray for people. You could participate with others, but you were also allowed to watch. If, however, you claimed to believe in Jesus, the motto was "Go big or go home!" There was no compromise. We were going to "go for the jugular" and find out if God was real or not. Over the years we did this, we saw some amazing things happen through the simple prayers of the most ordinary, natural people.

One night in particular stands out for me among many memorable gatherings. We had just concluded our opening time of worship, spread around tables and chairs throughout the auditorium. I proceeded to do what was fairly common practice for us after the first worship set. I sat on my stool and remarked, "Whenever we come together like this, God is always at work among us. Let's find out what he is doing." I briefly explained the concept of spiritual gifts for those who were new – that God loves to release supernatural enabling in these gatherings so that we can partner with him to see the miraculous take place.

"It is not uncommon," I said, "to have God's Spirit give people knowledge about what it is that he is willing to do or provide encouraging invitations from his heart that apply specifically to different individual situations here in the room." After encouraging them that it was okay to practise these things, that utilizing spiritual gifts did not have to be like rocket science at first, I asked, "What do you think God is doing and saying tonight?"

Most nights, a number of different people would give what are often termed "prophetic words." (We never actually used the "P" word because it added unnecessary baggage for some – they would be tempted to become much more religious and "otherworldly." It's much like calling people elders: They are doing just fine "elding", but as soon as they are given the title, they battle with a strong inner desire to print up T-shirts!) After each expression of God's invitation (things like, "God specially wants to encourage someone who has battled deep depression this week, with a number of sleepless nights. This is what he wants to say to you …"), I would ask, "Who is this word for?" If someone said, "That word is for me," I would ask them to share its significance. This would always bring great encouragement. It was so special to see how God would speak specifically to people and use us to do it.

We would then match up the people giving the revelation with those who identified with it and release everyone to pray for that need. At the end of a considerable time of prayer, we would report back on what God had done. This feedback would encourage our faith as well as help us adjust, learn and grow. During this season, we experienced many powerful healings and people coming to faith in Jesus as a result.

This particular night, when I asked the group what they felt God was doing, a girl in her late teens or early twenties who was relatively new to our service stood up and said, "I had a picture while worship was taking place. I saw a man's left hand and in his left hand the first two knuckles were all crushed and pushed to the side." My first thought was, "Great, that's an easy one. There are usually at least two or three people with crushed knuckles who come to our services at any given time." Actually, what I really thought was this, "Oh no, I'm afraid that she may have overextended herself. It's much easier when they begin with more general expressions like, 'I have an impression ... does someone here have a back?' Those are easy to match people up with for subsequent prayer." I made a mental note to encourage her later because I didn't have much faith that her revelation was accurate.

Our whole purpose in having these meetings was to risk trying to hear from God, so I asked, "Is there anyone who has this problem with their left hand?" Almost immediately a young man sitting at the very back of the room put his hand up. He had arrived halfway through the worship, brought by a worker from the drug and alcohol rehabilitation centre where he was staying. He had recently been released from prison and was not particularly enjoying his first worship service. To be more accurate, he had spent the last half an hour mocking the expressions of worship that he saw around him.

He had no idea what was really going on or what was about to happen. He did know, though, that the first two knuckles of his left hand were crushed (they had been injured in a street fight some years before) and the injury prevented him from opening and closing his hand. His acknowledgement did not reflect any faith or eagerness on his part – the sneer on his face said it all. Because I knew what was going to happen next – we were going to match those who had revelation with those the revelation was for and then release everyone to pray for those situations – I was somewhat hesitant, wondering how I could protect the young, innocent girl who had given the word.

During this practice session, there were a number of words of invitation that we believed were from God. We took some time to match everyone up, trusting that God would now release gifts of faith, power and healing. I noted carefully the group that gathered around this young man, determining to get to them quickly to encourage and console them. When I did get to them, what I saw was a pretty discouraged group. In the centre was a belligerent young man, sneering and staring at a small, terrified band of would-be pray-ers. They all had their heads bowed and their eyes closed – and it wasn't out of a sense of reverence. They were completely intimidated!

I made a mental note to gather the group after the service to encourage them not to abandon kingdom ministry entirely over one bad prayer time. In the meantime, I attempted to salvage the best of a bad moment. I pleaded with the man to try closing his eyes and with the group to open theirs. "Try to see what God is doing as you pray," I said, "instead of only observing what he is evidently not doing. Perhaps pray one more time – who knows what God may do." With that I moved on to the next team. Even I was discouraged.

What I did not know was that these simple words encouraged them enough to rally and pray once more. Very soon some startling things began to take place, noticed at first only by the young man being prayed for. His body temperature started to rise until his whole body was perspiring. This confused him because no one else seemed to be affected by the obvious overheating in the room. Next he began to feel a tingling in his body, a slight current that grew more and more intense until he began to fear that he was being electrocuted. This current moved through his body and down into his arms. Finally it shot down into his hand – the one with the injured knuckles.

What happened at that point astonished him. He heard a distinct cracking sound (though I don't believe any of the others heard anything) and then, to his amazement, his knuckles reformed perfectly so that he could move his hand freely. As he stood there, incredulously opening and closing his hand, he responded rather reasonably: He opened his mouth and began to swear! His whole worldview had just been blown away.

It's hard to know who was more surprised – the young

man or the people who were praying for him. There was, of course, great celebration on their part. Yet this was not the end of the story. At this point, the young woman who had the original picture of his condition stood in front of him and began to speak directly to him. She was trembling physically, some of which was the result of God's power resting on her, but most of which was simple anxiety since she had never done anything like this before. She looked intently at him and said, "When you were six years old, you were sexually abused." She proceeded to identify the man who had abused him. She then related to him a number of details of his earlier life. He went white as a sheet. This could only be God speaking to him. Finally she added, "... and God is inviting you to come to him." The young man gave his life to Jesus that night.

REACHING INTO THE TOOLBOX

Isn't that amazing? What is even more surprising is that it involved ordinary people, none of whom had international ministries or television programmes. This miracle occurred largely through the obedience of a young girl who didn't fully understand what she was doing. She just reached for the kingdom (what God's will might look like for this person), groped around a little and, with the help of the Holy Spirit, found God's hand. God put in her hand a tool, a supernatural tool, a spiritual gift and suddenly she was able to do something she could never have done in her own mind or strength.

This kind of experience is what God has invited us to share. He has invited us to reach consistently into his lavish toolbox and pull out supernatural tools that enable us to do what we cannot do naturally, and yet do it in a seemingly very natural state. The woman in our story didn't go into some kind of trance. She was absolutely in her normal mind. Joining God in his work isn't some kind of robotic experience, where we are overcome by a spiritual power that takes control of us so that we are simply a passive instrument. Sometimes what we experience isn't at all similar to the end result of our cooperation. In this case, even though the man experienced significant spiritual power in his body, the young woman hardly "felt" anything. In all that she said and did, she was completely conscious and in control of her faculties.

A DIVINE PARTNERSHIP

The first thing we must understand about spiritual gifts is that they are realized within a real partnership with God. It is neither 99% God and only 1% of a partially conscious us, nor is it 99% our effort and 1% of God helping out. It is a partnership in which we never know the exact combination of God's grace and our faith. We do know this: We cannot do it without him and evidently, most often, he will not do it without us.

Paul, the notable first-century church planter and leader, discusses how this partnership works in his letters to the believers in Corinth and Rome. In 1 Corinthians 12:1 he raises the issue of what he calls "spirituals", intentionally emphasizing that they are divinely rather than humanly initiated. In verse 4 he uses a slightly different term that means "gifts of grace" so that we would understand clearly that these gifts are not earned in any way. The context here is the receiving of these gifts in the gathered setting of the church ("when you come together"), gifts that are released in a specific situation of ministry, what John Wimber called "situational anointings". Paul explains that these gifts of the Spirit always come as a result of an interaction between grace on God's part and faith on ours. In verse 11 he states clearly that the Holy Spirit sovereignly distributes these gifts and "he alone decides which gift each person should have".

This is not to say that we should become passive participants with God, leaving the distribution of gifts entirely up to him. Paul explains later in the letter, but within the same context (14:1), that we should desire these gifts ("eagerly desire" NIV). In the New Testament, receiving the Spirit is always an active process. Similarly, spiritual gifts are not a badge for the mature but a response to the eagerly receptive. Paul makes it clear that no one person will have all the gifts. We will always need every part of the body of Christ, the gathered church, working together to see God's work accomplished (the Holy Spirit will safeguard that in his distribution of gifts). But we are to test God's generosity and seek the fullest expression of his gifts in and through our lives.

In his letter to the Romans, Paul discusses the same issue within a somewhat different context. The setting here seems more focused on our ongoing life of service to God. God gives us "the ability to do certain things well" (Romans 12:6). We see the essential partnership of grace and faith in a new context. These ongoing gifts, which seem more "natural" in that we feel that we have greater control over them, are also determined by God ("according to the grace given us" NIV). Faith on our part is an essential key. We are to use the gifts "in proportion to [our] faith" (NIV).

Both parts, God's grace and our faith, are essential in this spiritual partnership. Each situation may reflect varying proportions – some may seem to require a high degree of faith while others seem to be largely grace. I know how we want the partnership to work. We want a whole lot of "anointing" early on in the process, a lot of grace kicking in fast, with us exercising a minimum of faith – and that at the last possible moment! That makes sense, doesn't it? If we are going to give something away, we want to make sure we have a lot of it first. But is that what we can expect if we say "yes" to joining God in his work?

John Wimber often shared his insight into that question. He was often asked, "How do you know when you are anointed to pray for the sick?"

"First of all," John would respond, "you start to get a rubbery feeling in your legs, often followed by intense perspiration, mostly from nervous anxiety. Next, you can expect your tongue to feel very thick. This makes it difficult to say even your own name – which is fine, because your mind will have begun feeling so clouded that you will have difficulty even remembering your own name. When you start feeling these things, you can be really confident, because 'the anointing' is on you. You are ready to pray for the sick!" John's point was that "anointing" feels like an anxiety attack, because we have decided to take the risk of cooperating with God. But we don't really want it that way.

Jackie Pullinger-To, a woman from Hong Kong who has developed a powerful community among the poor in that city, has great authority in this area of faith and trusting God for provision. "If we wait until we have enough," she told me, "we will never give. But if we give what we have, we will not only have enough, but we will have a surplus." It certainly works that way with respect to spiritual gifts. Our tendency is to wait for sufficient anointing that will eliminate the risk of faith and "guarantee" our success. "Receive and you will be able to give out of your abundance," is the invitation of many conferences. While there is some truth to that, the biblical order seems somewhat different. "If you give, you will receive" (Luke 6:38), originally spoken by Jesus in the context of forgiveness, applies to all his provision.

God calls us to give and as we give, we receive. In the same measure we give, we receive. In response to his disciples, who were asking: "We need more faith, how can we get it?" (Luke 17:5), Jesus replied: "If you had faith as big as a mustard seed, it would be enough, just start investing it." Just start giving away what you have – that is really the way to grow in doing the Father's works.

Yet we constantly think or at least hope that there is a different way. We wish that someone could just pray for us and their "anointing" would come upon us – then we could easily do the spectacular things that they seem able to do. Years ago at a pastors' conference, John Wimber stopped in the middle of his message and said to the large crowd, "Many of you want to know the secret of how I operate in spiritual gifts. I will tell you right now exactly how I do it." There was an immediate stir throughout the room and a sudden surge of interest.

"As soon as you walk out of this session," John shared, "watch for any situation in which you feel that God wants you to join him. Whether what is needed is simply kindness or revelation or prayer – give whatever you feel the

Holy Spirit provides you." Then John continued, "After that, look for the next situation that seems to you to be one that God cares about and do the same thing." John repeated this two or three more times. By the time he was done, most of the crowd had stopped taking notes – this information didn't seem like much of a secret at all. In this teaching moment, John said, "All of you want to be where I am now; none of you wants to start where I started." It all begins with giving what we have.

WE OBEY, THEN GOD ACTS

I know we want a different process. We want something far stronger, something that we can control, some kind of formula we can apply. But this is far too dangerous. Consider the wreckage of lives that have become consumed with their own success and power. God loves us too much to let us be in control. That is why he has designed a process that is centred in weakness and requires total dependence on him – not simply until we have learned how to do it, but always. That's the way life works in the kingdom: God speaks, we obey, then God acts making the impossible possible.

This process doesn't fit naturally with my make-up and background. Perhaps that explains why I took a long time even to understand it. (I am from a German family and Germans, as you may know, like control. They like to cross their t's and dot their i's, not to mention crossing *your* t's.) Early on in my journey to step out and actively risk reaching for spiritual gifts, I kept waiting for God to give me the gifts I needed so that I could use them. However, nothing seemed to come, so I waited and complained. In one of my,

"Poor me, why are you holding out on me?" sessions with God, I had what I can only described as a divine daydream. The daydream was my own, yet I had a sense that God was directing it in order to speak to me.

In the dream, I was dialoguing with God, complaining to him about how hard it was to activate spiritual gifts in my life. He drew me into a memory that had always brought anxiety. He reminded me of an experience on a high diving board. I mean the particularly suicidal diving boards that you find at some Olympic-sized pools. They are approximately sixty-six to sixty-seven levels high, requiring oxygen tanks to ascend them. I once scaled one of these monsters. I remember vividly climbing through the clouds, seeing the wind gauge on the top tower (a foolish diver who did not take the wind velocity into account would have no hope of dying from contact with the water; he would land outside the pool) and noticing the binoculars hanging on the side (used for spotting the pool hundreds of metres below). I remembered "the feeling", that gnawing tumult in the pit of my stomach that told me, "Never, ever go near the edge of that platform, let alone act on a crazy death wish and actually consider jumping off the end of it."

In my daydream, I sensed God say to me, "This is what it is like just before you are about to have your faith and gifting grow."

"How wonderful!" I responded. "That feeling I know. But how will I actually get them to grow?"

I felt God say to me, "Look over the edge of the board."

"There's no water in the pool," I said, putting down the binoculars.

"Perfect!" God said. "Now, trust me and jump and I'll fill the pool with water."

"Can you do that?" I queried.

"Read the Book," God replied. "I am very good with water. It's one of my specialties."

I realized that this was a daydream – even if God was using it. But I decided to play along, even though I was experiencing a fairly intense degree of "the feeling". In my mind, I took two steps as though I were about to jump, but quickly stopped and looked down.

"What are you doing?" I imagined God saying.

"Working on my approach," I replied.

"No, you're not. You're checking to see whether I've started filling the pool. This is the way it works: You leave the board, *then* I fill the pool with water."

Only when the process works this way is our trust fully in God and his generous provision rather than in ourselves.

The Book of Acts gives us a glimpse of the first followers of Jesus. Even a surface reading of the letters written to the churches during that time shows that there were many problems, but there were many things they got very right. They demonstrated a powerful trust in God's faithfulness and provision. Acts 4 records an early time of intense persecution and opposition. The still fragile, inexperienced church community was challenged by the powerful, intimidating religious and political rulers, demanding that they cease speaking about this man Jesus, let alone doing the things he did.

Later in Acts 4, when Peter and John returned to the other believers and recounted the threats made against them, they all turned their voices toward heaven and cried out to God. What did they say? While affirming their commitment to "jump" in obedience to Jesus' command, they pleaded with God faithfully to "fill the pool with water". "Oh Lord, hear their threats," they said. "See the opposition of both these people and the demonic principalities and powers behind them and (this is what we ask you) give us great boldness, courage to obey – just give us courage! But as we do, will you stretch out your hand with miraculous signs and wonders done through the name of your Holy Servant Jesus (i.e. will you fill the pool with water?)."

Evidently, God liked that prayer, because he shook the whole building. We get excited when a few people shake. How would you like the whole building to shake? We obey, then God acts.

WHAT DID JESUS DO?

We might still ask: "What does obedience look like practically? Is there an example we can follow that would make the task of obedience a little clearer?" The recognizable bracelet, WWJD (What Would Jesus Do?), points to the same place that the New Testament does – the example of Jesus. That is a great place to start. Because he is our model, he is our example of how to live this life of faith. Jesus was fully God, but he was also fully human. In becoming human, he limited himself and operated in the same way he expects us to: Through complete faith, trust and dependence on the Father.

What, then, did Jesus do? In the first chapter, we noted from John 5 that Jesus did only what the Father was doing; he did nothing on his own. If we break that down, we realize that, in a very practical sense, Jesus' entire ministry rested on two things. First, Jesus listened – he always listened. He listened to people, but in listening to them, he was always listening for his Father's voice. We see in John 5:20 that, out of the Father's love for the Son, he told him everything that he desired to do. Jesus knew he could rely on the Father to tell him what he was up to. So he always listened to his Father's voice.

Jesus often drew aside from all the commotion to listen to the Father's heart for the coming events of the day. At times he seemed to walk into situations knowing what was going to take place. At other times, he didn't seem to have that kind of advance information. In those situations, he listened in the moment, relying on the step-by-step leading of the Holy Spirit. This didn't preclude asking people for information; he often asked specific questions about the history and nature of a situation. Yet he always kept an ear tuned to the Father and his direction in every circumstance. Jesus constantly listened.

The second key or foundation of Jesus' ministry was this: He simply obeyed what he heard. "I do nothing on my own," Jesus said (John 8:28–29), "but I speak what the Father taught me. For I always do those things that are pleasing to him."

"I don't speak on my own authority. The Father who sent me gave me his own instructions as to what I should say. And I know his instructions lead to eternal life; so I say whatever the Father tells me to say!" (12:49–50). Jesus didn't ask, "Will people like it?" or "What will be the consequences of what I say?" He trusted the Father completely for all of that. All he concerned himself with was, "Is this the Father's voice? If so, this is what I'm going to do; this is what I'm going to say."

Because of this complete trust in and obedience to his Father, the Spirit was able to fill Jesus without measure. There was no limit to the degree to which he could be anointed and filled by the Spirit, because there was no separation between him and his Father's will (John 3:34).

This literal, step-by-step obedience seemed to direct not only what Jesus chose to do, but also the way in which he did it. Take, for instance, his healing of blind people – a fairly common occurrence in his healing activity. Imagine for a moment that you are a reporter for the *Jerusalem Morning News* and your editor sends you to investigate the spectacular rumours emerging about the hot, new prophet from Galilee. Your editor's brief is: "I want you to write an article that outlines just how he does what he does. Don't miss anything. I want his secret method."

When you finally track Jesus down in Capernaum, it is your good fortune to find a crowd around him. He is about to heal two blind men. "How will he do this?" you wonder. As you watch and take notes, Jesus reaches out his hands to touch them. Then he says something about their faith (which you can't quite hear), touches them and then (it is simply amazing) these guys are saying, "I can see!" How did he do it? He simply touched them. You write down "touch". Where did he touch them? It looked like he touched them on the eyes. "I will have to take more notes later," you decide.

The next significant stop is in Bethsaida. Predictably, Jesus is healing many different people. Inside you are encouraging, "Find some blind people!" Soon your wish is granted; Jesus encounters a blind man. You watch intently. "I bet he is going to touch him," you say confidently. Jesus initiates a conversation and is getting into healing mode (rolling up his sleeves, etc.). Next, surprisingly, Jesus seems to be trying to clear his throat (perhaps he is getting a cold). Then he spits. That, in itself, may not be too shocking – people spit a lot in that part of the world. The disgusting thing is that he spits right in the guy's eye! And the guy couldn't even see it coming! To top it off, Jesus doesn't even apologize. Nor does the man seem to be offended – he can see! "Now that was weird," you say, not even knowing whether to write down what you just saw.

Some time later, while you are waiting for the next ministry time, you check your notes: "Touch" – check mark; "spit" – question mark; "a final prayer" – done! You're going to need some more examples to be sure you're right. Soon Jesus obliges you. You are now in Jerusalem and Jesus has encountered a man who has been blind from birth. As you flip open your notebook, you heard a familiar sound: Jesus is clearing his throat again! You want to warn the man, but it is too late. Thankfully, this time Jesus misses the man, but what happens next is beyond belief: Jesus picks up his grimy spittle and rubs it in the man's eyes – dirt and all. Then, rather than help the man wash it out, he sends him to the nearby pool of Siloam to do the cleanup himself. Before you can register your disapproval, however, as soon as this man washes, he too can see!

By this time you are observing, "Well, it is unusual, but there are good results. This seems to be the method: If there is more than one, or perhaps if they haven't been blind long, a simple touch will do. More serious cases, though, require spit. This man probably has magic spit; you need to get it in their eyes. This will make a great story!

It is with this certainty that you experience one last encounter of Jesus with the blind. There is quite a commotion involving a man named Bartimaeus. Apparently Jesus' disciples felt he was too busy and were trying to quiet the poor man. Your excitement grows when you notice that first, he is blind and second, Jesus evidently wants to heal him. You wait for the touch, for the sound of him clearing his throat. But Jesus doesn't touch him, he doesn't spit, he doesn't even pray for him. He just says, "Your faith has made you well. Have a good day." The man, of course, can see. You, on the other hand, have become increasingly blind – if there is a secret to Jesus' healing method, you certainly can't see it!

IMITATING JESUS

While there can be helpful teaching that enables us to learn and grow in praying as Jesus did, there is no method that will enable us to control the process. The only model we are given by Jesus is one of simply learning to listen to the Father and obey him. The risk lies in the fact that, quite frankly, we don't hear the Father's voice as clearly as Jesus did. Beside the reality that being the sinless Son of God has distinct advantages, we have all compromised our spiritual ears over the course of our lives by listening to many other voices. It takes consistent practice and discipline to tune our ears and wills to the Father's frequency.

It should encourage us that some of Jesus' early followers were also slow learners. Peter seems to have had some early difficulties distinguishing between his own impulsive desires and God's voice (Matthew 16:13–23; Luke 9:33–35), but over time he learned to hear that voice with powerful clarity.

As God showed him his own great weakness and vulnerability, he became a much better listener and his natural impulsiveness grew into a mature expression of faith. The result, that emerged at Pentecost and continued to grow, was a man who learned how to listen and obey just like his mentor (Acts 3:4–8; 9:39–41).

This simple approach of Jesus and his followers is the key to natural people like us partnering with the supernatural and seeing the same works of power that they did. Of course, we should use this key with humility. Like Peter, we can often mistake our own impressions for the voice of God. Therefore it is very important to take these risks of faith within a mature and supportive community. We hear and grow in our hearing best within relationship with and accountability to others. We should also sink our roots deep into the Word of God, which is the plumb line that guards against false revelation. With these provisions, however, a simple process of "listen and obey" can protect us wonderfully from our own pride by keeping us dependent on God. Trusting dependence is at least part of what Jesus had in mind when he said that "anyone who becomes as humble as [a] little child is the greatest in the Kingdom of Heaven" (Matthew 18:3).

THE RAW MATERIAL FOR A MIRACLE

The powerful potential of childlikeness is vividly illustrated in a story about Jesus recorded in Mark's Gospel (6:30–44). As Mark tells it, the disciples had just come back from their tremendous healing trip. They were excited about the amazing things they had seen and experienced. It had been a bittersweet time for Jesus. Countering his delight in his followers' good reports was the distressing news that his cousin, John the Baptist, had just been executed. While the disciples were trying to share the highlights of their tour, others pressed in on them, clamouring for ministry. The situation in the room could best be described as bedlam. When Jesus said, "You know what? We just need to get away for a while. I know about this great resort where there are lovely sailboats, not to mention a golf course. I tell you what guys, let's jump on the ferry, head over and take the weekend off. We'll have time to kick back and share about these things." He hadn't even finished this sentence and the disciples had their bags packed.

So, Mark reports, "They left by boat for a quieter spot" (v. 32). At least, they thought it was a quieter spot. Little did they know that someone had done their homework, the cell phones were buzzing and crowds were already beginning to converge on their retreat destination. I don't suppose the disciples were aware of this. I can envision Peter on deck practising his backswing, enjoying the fresh air and thinking, "This is going to be such a great time. We've earned it and now we're really going to enjoy it."

However, as they got closer to the dock on the other side of the lake, it looked like more than just the hotel staff were waiting for them. In fact, they realized that the crowd was not connected to the hotel at all. Instead, what they saw was a large group of people, all holding up big signs saying: "I Need". Have you ever been in that place? What did the disciples do? I imagine them looking at the people, then looking at their golf clubs, then looking at Jesus and finally looking at Jesus looking at the people. Sadly, they put their clubs away remarking, "He is going to do it again, isn't he?"

What Jesus saw was not an aborted holiday plan. He saw the people and how harassed and helpless they were, like "sheep without a shepherd" and he had great compassion for them. He sat them down and taught them all afternoon. The poor disciples had to wait a long time for their well-deserved rest to begin. Having heard a lot of Jesus' messages, they were most likely looking at their watches, trying unobtrusively to encourage him to get to the punch line with a segue into the prayer ministry time. Jesus, however, didn't seem to be getting the message. (Editor's note: Our present author has been known to read his own personality into the text at certain points. Let the reader beware.)

Late in the afternoon, they had an idea. They went to Jesus with deep compassion that they had recently discovered: "Jesus, this is a desolate place. Philip, as you know, is from this area. He knows the restaurants in the area – there simply aren't many. There is really no place for these people to eat and it is getting very late. So send them away! Then they can get something to eat and be taken care of." This seemed to make sense to Jesus. Maybe he had been so busy teaching, he hadn't noticed the time.

Jesus' response was a little surprising, though: "You feed them." (We may want to take a moment to underline that statement in our Bibles – we would do well not to forget that brief statement as the disciples quickly did.) We know from John's Gospel that Jesus knew something was up. While he was teaching, he had been listening at the same time and the Father had told him that he had something very special in store. The disciples, of course, were not aware of this. Their response to Jesus' instruction was incredulous: "Feed them? There are probably five thousand men alone! It could literally take a few months' wages to feed them all. We could actually give this money to the poor. We really shouldn't spend all this money on people who could just go home."

This stewardship angle seemed to work. Jesus asked, "How much food do you have?" Whatever the various possible answers to that question, they could all probably be summarized, "Not enough!" It was late in the day. Most likely any food that Jesus' audience had brought had already been eaten. (I have no doubt that the disciples, in their frustration, had eaten theirs.) At any rate, Jesus asked them to find out what was available.

The disciples were encouraged: All they had to do was find *some* food. By definition, what they found would not be enough and their vacation could begin. They could bring it back to Jesus and say, "We have done our part, but there is not enough, so send them home. There is simply not enough food." With this new vision, they began to search. Eventually they found a boy who had not yet eaten the meal he had brought with him. This was something of a surprise.[2] In spite of the fact that he himself would be quite hungry at that hour (growing boys nearing their teens always have substantial appetites), he willingly gave the disciples what he had brought.

---

[2]Jesus' listeners lived in a subsistence culture. Most were fortunate to eat two meals per day. Often those meals would consist only of bread and water with some oil for dipping their bread, if indeed that were available. Having fish with their evening meal was by no means a certainty. For the growing young man of this story (who would have had a healthy appetite), to have delayed eating what would have been a better than average meal, would seem to indicate that he was either very sensitive to those around him, very attentive to Jesus' teaching or, possibly, in some way he didn't even fully understand, he was being prepared by God for the miracle that followed.

How large was this meal? Five loaves and two fish! On his way out of the door that morning, his mom no doubt said, "Son, where are you going?" Perhaps he replied, "Jesus has just come across the lake and I want to go to hear him." I don't think she said, "Then just wait a moment, I'll pack you a meal for five thousand." This was made for him alone. How big were these loaves? These were little loaves – the size of dinner rolls or smaller. This was his lunch! The fish were like two little sardines.

By now it was late afternoon in the hot sun. When the disciples opened the bag to take a look, they most likely closed it quickly. "Thankfully we won't be eating that!" Triumphantly, they brought their trophy to Jesus. "This is it! We found a boy's meal." To which Philip added, "But what good is that?" Jesus seemed to be convinced. He instructed the disciples to seat the entire crowd in an orderly fashion so that he could direct them further. The disciples responded eagerly with a renewed glance at their golf clubs. At that point, Jesus started to break the loaves and the fish, asking God's blessing on the food. I can see Peter saying, "Jesus, I know that you've certainly earned it, but isn't it rude to eat in front of these hungry people? Shouldn't you dismiss them first?"

I don't know exactly when they got it. As Jesus broke the loaves and looked at them, then smiled, looked at the loaves again, the crowd, the disciples – at some point Peter began to do the same – loaves, crowd, Jesus, loaves, crowd. Eventually, they got it: "You want us to take this to them!"

At this important juncture in the story, there is a critical question that urgently cries out to be answered: Did the food multiply and, if so, when did it do so? I know when

the disciples would have wanted it to multiply: In Jesus'
hands before it got to theirs. Unfortunately, we can't answer
that question conclusively on the strength of the text alone.
Certainly an early multiplication would require much less
faith, which would have made the disciples much more
comfortable with their task. I suspect, however, that the
other possibility is the correct one: The food multiplied in
the act of the disciples giving it. (The stories I have heard
from friends who have personally experienced this miracle
definitely suggest this as the likely pattern.)

I imagine Peter standing with slightly less than half a
dinner roll and one-sixth of a sardine. (I like to think of
Peter getting the head.) Jesus looked at him, along with the
other disciples, and said, "All right, have a good time boys!"
Can you see Peter, hiding this less than ample banquet in
the palms of his hands, surveying the crowd? Which group
would he pick: The skinny ones or the fat ones? He had to
start somewhere. Eventually Peter and the others simply got
it over with. However apologetically, they offered what they
had to the first (and likely last) diner with closed eyes. As
they did, something happened – they opened their eyes and
that first person seemed to be munching on something, yet
they still had food in their hands to give! (Could it possibly
be more than before?)

Soon they realized a miracle was taking place. The
environment quickly became euphoric: It wasn't long before
food fights were breaking out, because with each act of giving,
there was more to give! Now remember, these were hungry,
rural people. There was enough food for a month, available for the taking. I'm sure they weren't worrying about
politeness. No doubt the mothers were stuffing extra into

their clothing to take home. Still, at the end of this wild time, there were twelve full baskets of food left over. The text doesn't tell us what they did with it. Was there one for each disciple to remember this miracle? Or perhaps they returned it to the boy, "Hey kid, here's your lunch back. Thanks a lot!" If so, what an investment on his part!

When did the food multiply? At least we know this: It did not multiply until they gave what they had. For this reason, the real hero of the story (other than Jesus) is the young boy. He had the trusting faith simply to give what he had. The disciples didn't offer anything – they decided that what they had wasn't enough. Unfortunately they had forgotten the most important thing: Listen and then obey. What did they neglect to hear? "You feed them."

Who is it that gave them this command? It wasn't simply Jesus the man speaking. The Father was speaking through Jesus, the Father who created all that is, the One who spoke but a word and worlds came into being. This is the One who said: "You feed them."

In response to this creative word, they could have offered anything and it would have been enough. They could have pulled out some lint from their pocket and it would have been enough. As far as I can understand, the only miracle in which something has been made out of nothing was creation. Ever since that time, all miracles have taken some kind of raw material. God had spoken; all they needed to do was to provide something and it would have been all that was necessary for everyone to go home happy.

What's the point? Simply this: If God has spoken and we are willing to give what we have, even our smallest act of obedience could be the raw material for a miracle. It is not about us and our capabilities. Doesn't that change everything? I think it does.

BECOMING LIKE A CHILD

When a number of my friends and I were first introduced to the miraculous possibilities of partnering with God, a certain wonderful naïveté directed our actions. All we knew was that the powerful God of miracles was on the loose and it was possible that even we could bump into what he was doing. As a result, our attention was intensely focused on trying to notice his activity in every circumstance.

While attending a conference in Southern California, we were learning about physical healing. Part of our learning experience was to practise what was being taught. That night John Wimber's guest had a sense that God wanted to bring healing to people that had a variety of alignment problems, all of which could be identified by the fact that one of their legs was longer than the other.

I was very aware that this was the case with me. For a number of years, Joy had been hemming one pants leg about three-quarters of an inch shorter than the other. Following instructions, I sat on a chair while a good friend and coworker, Andy Park, took note that, indeed, I did have one leg significantly shorter than the other. I was quite adamant that we not fake anything. I found it hard to believe at the time that something could actually happen to remedy my condition. If it did, I wanted to be sure that it was real (and not just Andy "pulling my leg"). Given my relative scepticism and unbelief, you can imagine the shock when I literally felt something tug my "shorter" leg and watched it seemingly change in length – even though Andy's hand was on the opposite side![3]

Seeing a number of these kinds of things happen to us greatly increased our general sense of kingdom expectation. This excitement and enthusiasm carried over from the sessions into our break and meal times. As we entered a restaurant to have dinner before an evening session, my friend Doug Watts leaned over to me and said, "Don't look now, but I'm convinced that the waitress behind the counter has one leg shorter than the other!" Our spiritual radar snapped into operating position.

The question was, "What to do?" How do you lead into a conversation that ends with, "So, is your one leg shorter than the other?" While we were pondering these complicated procedural matters, the waitress appeared and, sure enough, the way she walked gave it away: She did have one shorter leg! We had got the first part of the process (listen) right. Each of us gave the other a knowing look – God was obviously on the move! With great confidence, my friend explained to her something about our experience at the conference and concluded with: "God is healing today – especially problems like yours. If you will come over to our hotel room later tonight, we'd love to pray for you and God will heal your leg."

Later, when we looked somewhat more objectively at what we had said, we realized how unlikely it was that any self-respecting girl would show up within ten miles of our hotel. Just in case, we had our wives posted in the parking lot, ready to smile and reassure her that all was safe and legiti-

---

[3] I still am able to wear my jeans off the rack today without the need to re-hem one pants leg!

mate. Incredibly, around 10 p.m., she drove into the parking lot, bringing a friend for moral support and protection.

We were elated and quite convinced that we were on the edge of a miracle. Trying to follow the process, we began by asking her about her condition. "Yes," she said, "one leg is indeed shorter than the other – two inches to be exact." Two inches? We weren't sure God could do two inches! We felt we were in a little over our heads, but we couldn't turn back at that point. We simply began to pray as we were being instructed. "God, we believe that you gave us this revelation," we said. "Now will you do a miracle?" Within minutes of praying, her leg literally appeared to lengthen, though she hadn't in any way shifted her hips or adjusted her position. She was as shocked as we were! Encouraged by this obvious intervention of the supernatural, we began to speak to the leg and commanded it to continue to lengthen. Within a very short time, it continued to adjust until it was precisely the same as the other – two entire inches! Our new friend was beside herself, overwhelmed by what had happened.

At this point in our healing "careers", none of us really knew what we were doing and none of us felt particularly "anointed". We simply believed that if we could see and/or hear what God wanted to do, and did it, anything was possible. It didn't depend on us; it depended on God. Propelled by this belief, we simply but confidently began to reach for God's presence and work in every person and situation we encountered. As our simple faith grew, so seemingly did God's grace. Some months later, Doug and his wife Suzie saw, with their own eyes, a woman's foot grow two shoes sizes (though the woman herself was probably hoping to have the other foot shrink two sizes!). God was using our simple obedience as the raw material for miracles of his making.

READING THE WORDS, DOING THE WORKS

DISCUSS IT

What are some strengths you have that God may want to use?

- Help each other. As a group, point out each other's strengths.
- Make a list of ten ways or times God has used one of your gifts to bring his kingdom to a person or situation.

Have some fun! Dramatize the feeding of the 5,000 in a storytelling style to communicate Gary's point. Ask two people to retell the story. Highlight the strengths of each.

DO IT

In what ways do you long to see God's kingdom come?

- Pray about one or two of these specific desires with your partner.
- Make a commitment to listen to the Spirit this week and to obey each time you hear him give directions.

PRAY ABOUT IT

"O Sovereign Lord, Creator of heaven and earth, the sea, and everything in them ... give your servants great boldness in their preaching. Send your healing power; may miraculous signs and wonders be done through the name of your holy servant Jesus." (Acts 4:24, 29–30)

- Commit to continuing to pray for your prayer partner this week about his or her specific desires.
- Exchange phone numbers and connect during the week.
- Pray the prayer of the believers in Acts 4 for great boldness and obedience.
- Share next week what happened.

THINK ABOUT IT

Reconcile yourself with the fact that you will sometimes feel and look stupid if you do what is outlined in this book (Matthew 10:39).

CHAPTER 3

SEEING WHAT GOD SEES

In the last chapter, I used the metaphor of a divine toolbox to describe how God can provide us with the right supernatural tool to do his work in a specific situation. I emphasized that the tool selection process is always the product of a divine partnership of God's grace and our faith; although we are completely dependent on God for his divine enabling, we must actively reach for it. We will discuss now how these tools or gifts operate practically and try to uncover the key to using them successfully – with increasing confidence and frequency.

GIFTS IN A GATHERED CHURCH SETTING

Paul, the notable leader of the early church, provides our primary information concerning spiritual gifts and how they function. His most extensive teaching is found in his first letter to the Corinthian believers (chapters 12–14). This communication with the Corinthians is what is called an occasional letter – not because Paul only wrote occasionally (which may have been true because of the cost and effort of sending such an extensive manuscript), but because he was

writing to address directly a specific occasion, i.e. abuse of
the spiritual gifts in the church in Corinth. Paul's primary
purpose is to bring understanding and correction to their
existing practice.

This raises certain challenges for the modern reader.
First, we must attempt to reconstruct the questions and
issues from Paul's answers to understand fully the dialogue
that was taking place. Second, since he is not attempting to give a systematic, comprehensive teaching on this
topic, we must recognize that not all our questions will
be answered satisfactorily. As I mentioned briefly in the
previous chapter, Paul's teaching to the Corinthian believers regarding spiritual gifts specifically addresses the use of
gifts in the context of their gatherings (the clear context of
11:17– 14:40). We must therefore be careful in the way we
apply these principles to other settings.

Understanding the historical context of the Corinthian
church can help us to appreciate the challenge Paul faced
in discipling them. Gordon Fee writes in his excellent com-
mentary on 1 Corinthians: "Although they were the Christian
church in Corinth, an inordinate amount of Corinth
was yet in them, emerging in a number of attitudes and
behaviours that required radical surgery without killing the
patient. This is what 1 Corinthians attempts to do."[1]

In no way was Paul trying to restrict their practice of
spiritual gifts. Instead he was trying to correct a false notion
of spirituality that had resulted in their seeking of "prominent" gifts that would promote their status within the group.
He was attempting to put an end to a competitive spirit

_____

[1]Gordon Fee, *The First Epistle to the Corinthians* (Grand Rapids:
William B. Eerdmans, 1987), page 4.

that was actually inhibiting the development of the full spectrum of gifts necessary for the spiritual body of that community to be strong and healthy.

Not surprisingly, then, he begins by comparing the Holy Spirit's distribution of gifts in their gathered meetings to the relationship of diversity within unity found in the human body (12:14–26). What is Paul's point here? Is he trying to establish the concept of one member equals one gift, as many contemporary preachers have taught?

This view teaches that each part of Christ's spiritual body has a specific and unique function to contribute to the functioning of the whole (12:27–30). It tends to see gifts as innate endowments given at your creation or regeneration that need to be discovered and developed. It emphasizes learning to be content with the lifelong gifts you have been given. Of course, there is some truth in this. The danger is that it can create a passive or fatalistic attitude toward gifts that results in a specialization Paul certainly never intended. Immediately after emphasizing the diversity of God's distribution of gifts when the community comes together, he encourages them to "desire the most helpful gifts", apparently whether or not it seems to reflect their lifelong spiritual gift mix.

THE PURPOSE OF GIFTS

Instead of stressing one's lifelong, unchanging gifting, it appears that Paul's primary purpose in using the metaphor of the body is to counter the Corinthians' competitive sense of independence. Paul is saying: "Your whole focus needs to shift. No one person is going to have all the gifts in any setting. You need each other if you are to be Christ's body."

With this in mind, it is best to see Paul's various listings of spiritual gifts as illustrative rather than comprehensive. He most certainly isn't trying to finalize a hierarchy of gifting. Some of his lists are clearly "spiritual" (i.e. tongues, prophecy, miracles, healing, etc.), while others include what seem more like "natural" developed strengths (i.e. helping others, getting others to work together, etc.). Paul's point is to help the Corinthian church see that there is a vast array of "workings" of the Holy Spirit in and through them – almost everything has an element of the spiritual. The important thing is to use this entire, wide spectrum of gifts to serve fully and build others up.

Paul's advice is significant for us today. We fall prey to the same insecurities as the Corinthians and are tempted to try to lay hold of the most prominent gifts in an attempt to bolster our own sense of importance within the church. Paul says to us as well as them, "Keep your focus on serving others with all the grace that God supplies, fully expecting him to breathe on your seemingly natural abilities and empower them to produce supernatural results. *And* actively reach for every possible gift that is needed to build up the body – whether or not it feels familiar to you."

What a freeing thing it is to realize that God's grace is constantly working through us. It releases us from the comparison that begins when insecurity torments us. When we come together as a community and keep our focus on each other and on how we can support and strengthen the other instead of ourselves, we become a tremendous gift to one another from God's Spirit. Our cheerfulness, enthusiasm, hospitality or kindness will be used profoundly by the Spirit to heal and strengthen each other. And it will do so in a way that won't cause us to become puffed up with pride – we are just being who we are.

This soil of kind service is the perfect growth medium for the other "situational anointings" of revelation, healing and faith. Certainly that is why Paul inserts his comments about the centrality of love in this teaching. When we lack this love, the greatest supposed gifting can do more harm than good. When our foundational focus is on the Father's love, it releases a powerful flow of the Holy Spirit in and through us that makes everything we do supernaturally empowered.

Some years ago, I took a team of young people in their teens and early twenties to Europe, primarily to share at the annual conference of a Protestant denomination some of what we had been learning about joining God in his work. These young people wouldn't have described themselves as highly gifted (certainly not in a spiritual sense). About all they knew was that God had shown them his love and grace and they wanted to share his goodness with others in tangible ways. They were willing, not having well-established reputations, simply to give away what they had.

As we began our first main session, in a group of approximately two thousand people, I realized how intimidating it would be for our team. Most of those in the crowd were significantly older and they seemed quite conservative. I encouraged our team to stay focused on what God was doing (rather than what he wasn't) and simply to give what God gave them. "Our great encouragement," I told them, "is that we can't heal anyone. If anything is to happen, the critical factor will be God's faithfulness. What we can do, however, is love and then simply reach for all that God will gift us to do."

It is easier to say that than it is actually to do it. At the conclusion of my message, I felt that God gave me revelation of physical illnesses that he desired to heal. I was greatly encouraged that this revelation seemed to be accurate. People immediately responded and stood in the aisles. I had our team match with them and begin to pray for healing.

It was such a great meeting so far. The teaching had gone well, they had responded so easily to the gifts of revelation, prayer had begun. Then the first cause for concern began to emerge: None of the prayers were working! I had pre-arranged with our team that they would bring up anyone God touched to share what had happened as an encouragement. Some time went by and no one responded. I did everything I could to buy time, but eventually it was becoming obvious – nothing was happening! In spite of my song and dance, the audience was becoming impatient. I felt so badly for our team. They had given what they had, but it had not been enough.

Finally, just as the ushers were about to come to take me away, an older woman approached the stage and climbed the stairs to the microphone. Noticing a change in the faith posture of the group, I asked my interpreter what was happening. "She is an icon in this movement," he said, "and everyone knows that she is so crippled with arthritis that she could never climb those stairs without assistance." The woman shared how God's power had suddenly come upon her, strengthened her limbs and taken away her pain. The whole crowd was hushed. Almost immediately after this a leader in the movement announced that the deafness he had had in his left ear for the last seventeen years had been instantly healed. Many followed him to the microphone to share their healing experiences.

I estimated that well over fifty people were healed in that meeting. Our young team simply gave what they had in faith and with love. God responded to their obedience and gave them powerful gifts of healing. It is hard to know who was more excited – the recipients or the delivery people!

A LIFETIME OF SERVICE

In Paul's letter to the Romans, he says similar things within a somewhat different context. In this letter, he is dealing with specific issues that his missionary method might raise for the Roman church in preparation, hopefully, for his first visit. In chapter twelve, he again uses the metaphor of the human body to explain how we are given grace to serve one another in various ways (12:3–8). He emphasizes that these gifts result from a coworking of grace and faith. "If you sense God's Spirit at work in you," he says, "then exercise your faith and use that gift for the benefit of others."

The illustrations he then gives reflect the varied spectrum he uses in the Corinthian letter – one is more seemingly "spiritual" (i.e. prophecy) while others are very "natural" (such as giving or encouraging). In other words, throughout the course of our everyday lives, we are to expect and welcome the Spirit's grace to flow through us along the whole con-tinuum from the supposedly most natural to the most spir-itual. (Peter, one of the Twelve, gives very similar counsel in his general letter.[2] He encourages the recipients of his letter to look actively for the spiritual dimension of grace in their natural service to others, eagerly reaching for it by faith.)

---

[2] 1 Peter 4:8–11.

Gifts, then, are not confined to gathered settings of the church, when God's Spirit sprinkles his "gracelets" among his body. We can exercise our faith and reach for such gifts, even repeatedly the same gifts, in every setting of our lives over the long term. Joy has increasingly grown in the gift of generosity over the course of her life. As she has seen the wonderful fruit that it produces in others' lives, her desire and faith to give has continued to grow. Whenever she detects any balance in our bank account, her heart leaps. (Perhaps there is more to give!) As she reaches into her spiritual toolbox, it is seemingly quite simple for her hands to identify the tool of generosity.

Our daughter Jaana has grace from God to serve. As a midwife in the slums of the Philippines, she poured out her life for oppressed and disadvantaged mothers and children in ways that didn't, to my eyes, seem humanly possible. She never approached these extreme demands as an obligation. Instead, she saw them as a privilege. As a result, her service produced (as it continues to produce) a desire in those touched by her to serve in the same spirit.

Having seen the blessing and encouragement that healthy prophecy can bring to others, my friend Joyce has consistently searched in her toolbox for that particular tool. Her growing faith has enabled her to find it over and over again – to great benefit!

SPIRITUAL GIFTS IN THE MARKETPLACE

What about the operation of the Spirit's gifting outside the body of Christ? Are spiritual gifts only for building up one another within the community of faith? The answer of

Scripture would be an emphatic, "No!" While there is no direct teaching that addresses this issue, New Testament practice strongly illustrates that this should be an expected part of living out our commission as Jesus' apprentices.[3] Not only do the Gospels give example after example of Jesus exercising these gifts from the Father; the Book of Acts similarly documents the authority of the early believers to do the very same things as the Holy Spirit's grace empowered them. It was God's Spirit that anointed Jesus to seek after the lost (Luke 19:10). It was in those settings that his greatest miracles were seen. The apostles, likewise, saw miracles occur outside the gathering of the believers. In fact, perhaps the singular key to the rapid acceptance and expansion of the gospel was the Spirit's demonstrations of power through them (Acts 9:32–42). Later, Paul used similar gifts in his evangelistic work with great effect.

In the early 1990s, I took a team from our God Rock congregation to Denmark. We set up our band in the town hall square in central Copenhagen one evening. Getting noticed wasn't a problem. We had a sound system that could be heard in northern Germany. The question was what approach would be the best. Should we do a concert, hoping the lyrics of the songs would present a compelling message? Should we simply worship, trusting the Holy Spirit to attract hearts to himself? Should we preach a message so that the Good News was clearly portrayed? Or would the best option be a combination of the above?

---

[3]This is the subject of *Prophetic Evangelism* by Mark Stibbe, an Authentic Media publication.

SEEING WHAT GOD SEES

We decided to begin with worship and intersperse it with attempts to use whatever spiritual tools God would give us. Needless to say, it was a stretch for our faith. By the end of the first few songs, approximately five hundred people had gathered. The quality of the music fooled them: They hadn't yet realized that this was an "outreach". At that point, I took the microphone and explained that we were a group of Christians and that this was how we worshipped. Since I knew what most people were thinking, I simply acknowledged it. "I know that most of you will be tempted to tune out immediately (i.e. having been victims of 'outreach' before), but I want you to know that we are absolutely committed to the things we are singing. The love of this Jesus has made a radical difference to us."

While I was sharing this, I was frantically reaching around in the toolbox trying to catch hold of a tool from God that would show me what to do next. As I did so, a train of thought came to mind. Desperate, I went with it. "This city, perhaps more than any other in Europe, longs for love," I said. "Sadly, it has settled for far less." Then, certainly with some apprehension, I began to speak out the thoughts that were coming to my mind: Specific information about individuals that had gathered around us that underscored their deep hunger to love and be loved. I spoke directly to a couple that I believed had stopped to listen on their way to one of the many sex shows and began to describe some elements of their conversation along the way. "God is showing me this," I said, "because he wants to satisfy these longings of your hearts." Of course, on the one hand, no one could really know (other than the people I referenced) whether this information was true or not. However, what became obvious in the response of the crowd, was that the Holy Spirit was bringing his authority to support my obedience.

I repeated this process twice more during our time of worship. At the conclusion of our time, I told the crowd that our team would be delighted to speak with anyone who responded to what I had been saying and would pray with them. It was so encouraging for our team actually to pray for a number of the people I had spoken about and realize that God had used this revelation to prepare and soften their hearts. A number of people took a significant step toward the Source of love, including three young Muslim men who made a decision to become followers of Jesus.

GIFTS FOR A LIFETIME

What is common to all these settings? Is there a process common to both the immediate and the long-term, the marketplace and the gathered Christian community? John Wimber suggested a possible construct to explain the transition from gifts received "in the moment" to a lifetime of service.

The key to gifting begins with an intentional commitment to our role as Christians – practically endeavouring to practise the words and works of Jesus. When we step towards expressing the heart and will of God in this way, we soon encounter situations that require more than our own abilities. For instance, we can share the gospel with people, but we cannot provide the conviction required for repentance – it is a gift of the Spirit. We can pray for people to be healed, but for it to be effective, a gift of healing is required. Yet without fulfilling our role, we may never experience the gift.

John Wimber's wife Carol tells this story of an opportunity that presented itself to her and her sister Penny:

> We had been shopping together and were waiting in line
> to have lunch at a restaurant in the mall that we particu-
> larly liked. Though it was crowded, we felt it was worth
> the wait. While we were still fourth or fifth in line, our
> conversation was suddenly interrupted by a loud scream
> from one of the back tables: "My baby! I've dropped
> my baby! Help me!" The whole restaurant immediately
> hushed as an obviously distraught mother began to wail.
>
> Though we couldn't see over the crowd to know
> exactly what was going on, without even consulting each
> other, Penny and I immediately stepped into our role as
> Christians: We dropped our packages and rudely pushed
> our way through the line until we reached the table
> where the crying was coming from. What we found was
> a young mother who had been celebrating the arrival of
> her newborn child with some friends.
>
> When we quickly asked what had happened, she
> explained frantically that she had forgotten to connect
> the strap on the baby carrier so that when she lifted it,
> her six-week-old baby slid out, landing head first on
> the concrete floor. The child was unconscious, his face
> misshapen and already turning blackish. Instinctively,
> Penny and I laid hands on the child and boldly said to
> the mother, "We are Christians and we are going to ask
> Jesus to come here right now and heal your baby."
>
> "Yes! Yes! Please! Please!" the mother managed to
> gasp.
>
> We prayed confidently (and loudly, as I remember),
> blessing the life of this little one and rebuking the plan
> of evil. Somehow both of us knew that God had placed

us in the line at this restaurant for this very purpose: To stop this tragic event! By the time the ambulance arrived, the baby looked and sounded fine. At the same time, a sense of peace had come to the mother – she was smiling and relieved.

Later that day we received a message that the baby was given a clean bill of health without suffering so much as a bruise. As if that wasn't enough of a reward, the manager of the restaurant gave Penny and I a free lunch, after which we gathered up our packages and, feeling like Super-Grandmas, waved goodbye to everyone and went on with our shopping.

As this story illustrates, when we cry out to God for his gracious provision, we may have the experience of latching onto a supernatural tool, a spiritual gift that perfectly fits the required task.

What can happen over time, with repeated faithfulness on our part? We may repeatedly grasp the same tool until we gain some faith that God is particularly pleased to give us a certain tool again and again. As a result, eventually we may be drawn by our faith to those situations that require a certain kind of tool. When we reach into the toolbox, we may not just grasp the first thing that our hand touches – we search for what is, by now, becoming a familiar implement.

As this process repeats, our faith grows so much that it becomes almost second nature to expect God's faithfulness in this way. His grace seems to keep in step with our faith. It is not that we ever come to the place of possessing this gift – we are always utterly dependent on God and his mercy – but as our faith grows, we can access it more and more frequently. In fact, it may become so much part of our experience that others begin to recognize it as a ministry.

Of course, there is nothing wrong with this. It may well serve to increase faith and expectation in others, which is a good thing, as long as it is others who are identifying it as such. For me personally, there is nothing as tiring as people who seem to be obsessed with their "ministries". "Here's my card: John Doe – Prophecy and Intercession. Call me ..." What a sad thing that is!

GOD'S MAIL DELIVERY PERSONNEL

We would do well to remember that the word "ministry" simply means "service" – if we print up any cards, they should simply say, "John Doe – Servant". The whole purpose of these tools, as powerful as they are, is simply to empower us to serve. They are never intended to exalt us in any way or to be worn as badges of honour. In fact, they aren't really ever our gifts at all. They are packages of God's grace for others. We are just the UPS[4] messengers. What a wonderful "ministry" that is!

Because of God's mercy, we get to deliver the most incredible packages and as we eventually get them to the right people, we also share in their joy as they open them. When these people open the packages, they don't bow down in gratitude and chant, "Oh mailman! Oh mailman!" Neither do we expect a thank you card. We just delivered the package! Gratitude needs to be expressed to the giver of the gift. We should be thankful that we participate in such a wonderful process.

---

[4]UPS is the abbreviation for United Postal Service, a major North American courier service.

Sadly, it has almost got to the point that we can't safely use the word "ministry" anymore. It is almost like the words "elder" or "church". Such words become so abused that they communicate almost the opposite of their originally meaning to most hearers. They can never be used without an extensive explanation. With respect to spiritual gifts, we would be best advised to put "God's Postal Service" on our business cards and leave the language of "ministry" to others.

THE GREATER GIFTS

Paul was trying to convince the Corinthians to abandon this kind of self-focus that is fixated on your own "ministry". He wanted to dismantle their hierarchy of gifts, which was heavily influenced by the first seeds of Gnosticism and was promoting pride and competitiveness.[5] In its place, he was suggesting a different kind of ranking: He encouraged them to desire eagerly all of God's gifts, but especially the "most helpful" ones (12:31), i.e. those that build up others the most.

Does Paul give us any sense of what these "most helpful" gifts are? He does single out one gift (14:1). However, we may want to be sitting down and perhaps even fasten our seat belts before we hear what it is: The gift of prophecy! Any pastor that has been around awhile with some experience with this gift in the local church may be tempted to read that as a later addition to the text. If you are in leadership in

---

[5]For an analysis of Paul's refutation of Gnosticism in 1 Corinthians, and in other New Testament Books, refer to the Vineyard Bible Institute course by Derek Morphew, *The Spiritual Spider Web: A Study of Ancient and Contemporary Gnosticism.*

a local church, prophecy usually involves you in something of a love-hate relationship. It is the agony and the ecstasy: "Oh thank you, God, for prophecy!" or "Oh God, are you sure this was your idea?" Due to this experience, you would almost expect to read in 1 Corinthians: "Desire the special abilities the Spirit gives, [even] prophecy." If we were writing Paul's letter, we would express it this way: "Prophecy has got to be in there somewhere. Keep it in another room, but look, try to let it happen a little bit. The church is always supposed to be a little weird."

Why this reservation? Primarily because prophecy has always had a somewhat chequered history. Even at the time of the writing of the New Testament, problems had already emerged. Paul, writing to the Thessalonian believers, attempts to dissuade them from completely dismissing prophecy (1 Thessalonians 5:20). Why were his comments necessary? It seems that much of the prophecy in the Thessalonian church wasn't being very effective in building up the body. In effect, Paul was saying, "Don't throw the baby out with the bathwater. Test it, but hold onto the good and build from there." It sounds as though there might have been too many "ministries" and not enough "mail carriers".

Because of some of my early experiences with the prophetic, I had considerable difficulty seeing the merit of Paul's encouragement to desire prophecy most of all. However, being committed to the truth of God's Word, I realized that there had to be a baby somewhere in the tub. I'm pleased to say that, some years later, I can echo with conviction Paul's encouragement. I've had the privilege of seeing a strongly prophetic community of believers emerge with little of the weirdness often associated with this gift. I've been blessed to see people "naturally supernaturally" encourage others with tremendous effect – not even completely aware of the degree to which they were operating from supernatural insight because their focus was so completely on the welfare of the other.

It has also been a great joy to me to see the prophetic description in 1 Corinthians 14:24–25 being lived out. A short time after Jeremy (now our son-in-law) had surrendered his life to Jesus, he came to the Friday night congregation, God Rock. Within the first few weeks of attending, at least four or five different young people had come up to him, completely unaware that they had a developing ministry, simply seeing God's heart of invitation for him, and exposed the secrets of his heart (the theological expression is "read his mail"). While he had previously mocked these kinds of things, never having experienced them himself, the accuracy of these "words" impacted and attracted him. Now, years later, he is one of the more prophetic people that I know. He cut his spiritual teeth in the "postal service", where everyone was thrilled simply to deliver packages.

What is the key to seeing this gift take its proper place in such a healthy way? By keeping the main things the main things.[6] How does Paul describe the central characteristics of prophetic gifting in 1 Corinthians 14? The fruit that

---

[6]It is outside the scope of this writing to explore this topic in greater depth, though much more study is needed for a helpful understanding of prophecy, both biblically and experientially. I would recommend Bruce Collins's *Prophecy* (Berkhamstead: New Wine Publications, 2000) and *Prophetic Evangelism* by Mark Stibbe. They offer theologically sound and very accessible training.

best identifies healthy prophecy is that people are helped in their spiritual growth, particularly by being encouraged and comforted (14:3).

Our community tried to become very good at doing just these things. We asked God to sharpen our senses so that we could see what he sees, realizing that he is the God of invitation. We left the more exotic, eschatological musings to more experienced prophetic people with untimely births and uncommon gifting and tried to excel as a small "p" prophetic community – inviting and encouraging people to the wonderful invitation that God has for them.

PROPHECY IN THE CHURCH

Prophecy, when it functions this way, is a blessing in the church. When the gift is used with the right heart, it enables people to encourage one another at the deepest level. Of course, the body of Christ, when it is functioning well, is a naturally encouraging environment. However, often when we are especially discouraged or oppressed, it is difficult for this support to penetrate the resistance. The comfort we receive from others stays at the level of human comfort. This is important, but in our times of greatest need, human comfort itself is not enough. We need God's encouragement to touch our deepest fears and doubts.

Prophetic insight will uncover circumstances, expose thoughts and/or conversations that help the person realize that the encouragement that is about to come is truly from God; the one speaking/praying could simply not know these details. This is what I call the "calling card" phase of prophecy that makes clear to the one receiving the prophecy, "This is God speaking!"[7] Often the one praying or speaking isn't even fully aware of this: They are focused on engaging with God's heart for the other and are trying to deliver God's encouragement and invitation. Yet often they are using words and expressions that have great significance to the hearer, words that clearly indicate to the one being encouraged that God is speaking to them.

That is why we have to be very careful not to prejudge prophetic words. While they may not seem profound to us, they may have far more significance than we know for the ones to whom the Holy Spirit is speaking. Some years ago, I was invited to share with a small gathering (about fifteen people) of young developing leaders. As I did so, I had a strong sense (that I believed to be from God) that I should

---

[7]Jesus illustrated this in his dialogue with Nathanael, recorded in John 1:43–51. Jesus' insight into Nathanael's character was given greater authority in Nathanael's mind because of Jesus' ability to relate some information that he could not have known humanly – that is, where Nathanael was before Philip found him. In our experience, we have found that sometimes this revelation involves the naming of a physical condition that the person could not know without previous information. This revelation can help to release faith in the one who suffers from that condition: They recognize that God is already at work. Some years ago, in a ministry clinic time after a service, I had a distinct impression that a woman who had responded had a serious vertigo problem. This thought came to me immediately I saw her. Instinctively, I spoke this out over her before my natural hesitance could take control. At once, there was a visible outpouring of the Holy Spirit on her body. Later, debriefing her, I discovered that my words spoke very specifically to her physical condition and, knowing that only God could have shown me that, she was filled with hope and faith. Even better, some years after this experience, she was still absolutely free from what had been a serious, long-term problem.

give each of them a taste of the wonderful invitation that God wanted to extend to them. I knew that if I could catch hold of it myself, it would deeply encourage them.

With some hesitation, I began with the first person. Amazingly enough, he found my words very significant. I continued with one after the other until I myself was suitably impressed – I was sure I should take my newfound ministry on the road! I continued to be quite captured by my prophetic ability, when it seemed that God suddenly pulled the prophetic plug. I had come to the last person and, at that point, all "anointing" for prophetic insight dried up. Other than the thought, "God sees you as one who truly has integrity," nothing came to me. I couldn't even make anything up – my mind was blank. At the same time, I saw the hunger in his eyes and was very humbled and ashamed of how quickly I had begun to take credit for what had been purely God's gift. I so badly wanted to explain to him that the absence of encouragement for him was not his fault or God's but completely mine.

After doing so, I apologetically shared the seemingly insignificant word that I had for him. As I did so, I could see immediately that my words had impacted him. I asked him, "Does that word mean anything to you?" He responded, "You couldn't have known that for the last three or four weeks, I have been overwhelmed with condemnation. I have considered stepping out of all that I am doing, because I haven't felt that I have sufficient integrity. As a result, I have been daily asking God, 'What do you think?' This was his answer." Since then I have been very careful not to judge a prophetic word by the impression it makes on me. Perhaps it's simply a package intended for another person.

I could give hundreds of examples like this from my church experience. When followers of Jesus commit themselves to care lovingly, pray for one another and simply ask the question: "God, what is your wonderful invitation for my friend? How do you want to affirm and strengthen him?" the Holy Spirit is faithful in sharpening their natural encouragement with supernatural revelation. The result is divine comfort at a deep level of the soul.

PROPHECY OUTSIDE THE CHURCH

This gift, however, isn't just for the church. It is also a wonderful and powerful tool outside the church to bring genuine conviction. As already mentioned, Paul describes this dimension of the prophetic in 1 Corinthians 14:24–25. He describes how divine revelation can expose the hearts of non-believers in such a way that they exclaim, "This isn't just a bunch of people listening to bad sermons – God is in this place!" This was the experience of the young man who was dramatically healed in our God Rock service; the secrets of his heart were disclosed and he knew that he was truly encountering God.

Any of us who have tried to share God's Good News with others discover what the Scriptures say clearly: At times they seem spiritually unable to hear, almost as though something is blocking their ears or blinding their eyes, so that they cannot see its truth and benefits. Paul explains in 2 Corinthians 4:4 why this is so: "Satan, the god of this evil world, has blinded the minds of those who don't believe, so that they are unable to see the glorious light of the Good News that is shining upon them. They don't understand the message we preach about the glory of Christ, who is the exact likeness of God."

I remember a young woman steeped in New Age thinking, who was at first very antagonistic to the kingdom message. Eventually, and somewhat miraculously, she became a follower of Jesus. After some time of growing as a Christian, she shared with me, "I find it so amazing – what I am learning and experiencing is the exact opposite of everything I believed about Christianity. It is everything I ever wanted, but I could never see it previously!" Why was that? Satan had blinded her.

Often we cry out to God, "Would you reveal yourself to them? Would you penetrate this veil of blindness so that they can see how good you are?" Often, if we will listen, God will answer this prayer through our obedience. He will give us revelation that can penetrate their hearts and convince them that God is indeed speaking to them. This revelation can help them hear the rest of God's invitation with new ears. This is not just for the gifted that stand on stages. This is something every one of us can do – and the opportunity to do so can present itself at the most surprising times when we are the least ready.

A few years ago, I was introduced to a new friend who had begun attending our Sunday services through a relational connection with our son-in-law. He had a very troubled past and, as a result, had spent much of his adult life in prison for very serious offences. Many of these crimes were committed as a member of a well-known international biker gang. At first, the main point of his conversations centred on how he liked to hurt people (he was not a follower of Jesus at that stage). I kept wondering why he wanted to tell me this!

He was living in a neighbouring community, well known for its brokenness and crime. Since I had grown up in that community and was familiar with the violence that went with it, we had lots of common ground to talk about.

One Sunday he suggested that we get together for lunch to talk further about what our church could do to make a difference in that community – something I had a tremendous heart to do. He suggested we meet after the service in a biker bar where he and his friends spent most of their leisure hours. I agreed but decided to take along another friend for moral support. He was a new Christian and a police officer.

When we arrived at the parking lot, the friend I had brought along became quite uneasy. His familiarity with Hell's Angels bars told him that he didn't like our chances of having an uneventful lunch. When we got inside, I spotted my friend. However, this was not to be a quiet lunch alone. He had five or six of his friends with him. We had come to their church potluck!

The menu at this potluck varied slightly from the more churched versions: There was no food on the menu, only beer and cigarettes. A second notable difference had to do with vocabulary – there was a distinct pattern of every second or third word beginning with the letter "F". Thankfully, there were no strippers on Sunday, just an empty stage and pole.

Immediately my friend introduced me as his pastor. I introduced my friend the cop. This was too good for the group to pass up – a pastor and a cop in a biker bar. They immediately launched into conversation. We often wonder what topics are being discussed in those environments.

What do they want to talk about? Are they concerned with the problem of suffering or perhaps women in leadership? (Bikers meet the church: What is the question of the day?)

First they asked the cop, "Who do you like better, the new criminals or the old criminals like us?" (The right answer, of course, was the old criminals because the new ones have no respect.)

After this, a man caught my attention, looked intently at me and said, "I've got a question for you. Do you believe in UFOs?" Of all the questions I might have anticipated, I never expected that one.

"Well, this is God's universe," I stammered, "but it is a big universe and he could have a lot of stuff out there that I don't know anything about – so who knows."

He kept his eyes fixed on me and replied, "That was a trick question ... and you gave the right answer." From that point on, I was his buddy!

For the next hour or so, we had quite an animated discussion about many things. I quickly discovered that it was counterproductive to talk much about the church – surprisingly, it doesn't seem to have a very good reputation in biker bars. On the other hand, they loved talking about Jesus. They loved the stories about what he did in the Bible and similar things that I had seen him do. They especially loved stories of deliverance. ("Is that like the *Exorcist* with people puking and everything?")

At one point our discussion was centred on the healing that I had personally seen Jesus do. In the middle of this dialogue, two bikers next to me pulled out pictures of their mothers and said to me, "Would you pray for our mothers?" The great thing about this was that they had no idea what that might mean. I suppose they suspected that I might go home into some kind of closet filled with smoke and supply the suitable chants. Almost certainly, they would not be suspecting me to do anything right there and then.

In their invitation, I saw another – God was creating an opportunity to extend his invitation. Quickly, before my courage evaporated, I said, "I would love to pray for your mothers." I reached over to put my hands on their chests (and closed my eyes, because I simply didn't have the courage to leave them open) and started praying for their mothers. It was, however, one of those surreptitious prayers: "Oh God, bless their mothers," while I was frantically asking, "Oh God, just tell me anything about these guys that will show them that you know and love them."

Before I could second guess myself, I began to speak over them impressions that I hoped were from God about their earlier lives and some of their secret hopes and dreams. This wasn't really a legitimate prayer, more of a prophecy, but they didn't know the difference and besides, they didn't want to interrupt the holy man. After a few minutes, I closed the prayer with a blessing for their mothers (which in a biker bar is a long prayer!). It was then that I had a crisis of confidence. I suspected that bikers were not gracious receivers of inaccurate prophecies. Hesitantly, I opened my eyes only to see tears running down both their cheeks. "This is a holy place," I thought.

This soft response really encouraged me and strengthened my courage. I asked the man next to me, who was unemployed due to a serious wrist injury from a fall while he was drunk, "Could I pray for your wrist?" He had told me of his great concern over the likelihood expressed by his doctors that he would never be able to work again – he was a long-haul trucker.

"Not here!" he said, looking around. "I'll come to your church."

There is nothing like the sound of a Harley pulling up to church! After the service, which he and his wife found very interesting, I gathered a team of twenty-somethings to pray for his wrist. They gathered around him and repeated what I had done in the bar – they began praying over him God's wonderful invitation, ending by praying for his wrist. When they were finished, he literally couldn't speak. With tears in his eyes, he tried to describe, through gestures, the Presence that was resting on him. He discovered over the next few weeks that his arm was completely healed.

Some weeks later, we had this couple over to our home for dinner. After a great time eating together, we asked them, "Has anyone ever told you the whole story of this Book, the Bible, and how you can have an intimate relationship with Jesus?"

"No," they said. "Would you tell us?"

After an hour or so of sharing the incredibly Good News of the Bible, we had the privilege of introducing this wonderful couple to Jesus.[8]

This is the account of how Timothy Victor and Wayne Thornley, members of the New Song Vineyard in Cape Town, South Africa discovered God can work when we take risks and try to hear what the Father is doing.

---

[8]As a result of his healing, he got his job back and went back to the road. We eventually lost contact with them – thankfully God has not. When you hear great stories like this, please add your prayers to ours that God will wonderfully protect and complete the work he has done in these lives.

In 2002, we felt God was saying we should begin reaching out to people who are part of the New Age movement (we now call this ministry Developing Spirituality),[9] so we hired a stall at our local monthly New Age fair, The Holistic Lifestyle Fair, a gathering of clothing, food and trinket vendors and New Age spiritual practitioners of all kinds.

Our initial project was simply to be there, talk to people and hand out some reading material. If an opportunity for prayer came up, we would take it.

It was heavy going on a number of fronts, not least of which was the tremendous spiritual and physical pressure placed on our group by our stall neighbours, representatives of the Sahaja Yoga movement. They did not like what we stood for at all and, on more than one occasion, Tim found himself surrounded by them, with very aggressive questions being flung at him.

In late 2003, we decided it was time to offer a service that was similar to the psychics'. We wanted to bring Vineyard-style prayer ministry into the fair. We set up a new stall in a new location, this time sharing a large room with tarot card readers, palm readers, automatic writers and other psychics. We called the service Open Channelling – the closest New Age description of what we do with the Holy Spirit. Essentially it means talking to a spirit and expecting an immediate response.

On our first day, the going was slow. By 11 a.m. we had only seen about two people. Then a man came in looking like life had given him a good working over.

9http://www.developingspirituality.co.za.

SEEING WHAT GOD SEES

Tim was chatting to someone, so I went over to him. He read the pamphlet we had on the wall and asked me if we were Christian. I said we were. He looked like he had caught a whiff of a bad smell. He then asked if we tried to convert people. I told him we facilitated an encounter between people and God and what they did with that experience was up to them. Another bad smell.

I asked him if he wanted to give it a try. He said, "OK." He sat with Tim and me, and Tim started talking about what we do and some of the key points of worldview. At some point, Tim turned to me and asked if I "had anything" from God for the man. This was our little routine. I had nothing. Then I remember seeing the tiniest little thing and decided to talk anyway. I started with, "I see a house ..." and carried on from there. The man's eyes grew wider and wider and all the antagonism left him. When I finished telling him what I saw, he sat back in his chair and exhaled. He said something like, "That's amazing, because it is a house ..." and went on to describe how everything God had showed me was a description of his life. We prayed for him and he left.

A little while later a woman sat down at our stall. When we asked her what had brought her to us, she said something like, "Well, there's this guy out in the passageway telling everyone that you guys are amazing, so I thought I'd try it out."

From that point on a queue developed and we didn't really have a break for the next five hours. Towards the end of the day, we were exhausted. With every person who sat down, we were convinced that we would get nothing from God. It seemed, though, that as long as we were conscious and able to speak, God spoke. We received an average of three accurate words for every person we saw. We went home completely spent, but ecstatic.

At our second fair, we had an encounter with a tarot card reader. She was sharing the room with us. She came over to our stall right at the end of the day and sat down. In between "zoning out" and listening to her spirit guides, she said that she had been watching us all day and had been fascinated because the entire time she had seen a circle of powerful spirit beings standing around us. In the centre of the circle, she had sensed enormous love and peace and she had been desperate to "push into" the circle to find out exactly what was going on. While sitting with us, she zoned out again and then said, "You believe in the Three-in-One?" We said yes and she laughed and said, "Yes! That's what I'm getting!" As it turned out, she had encountered the Holy Spirit many years previously, and was very surprised to be seeing the same spirit again here.

Since then we have been running the stall every month with a growing number of people on our team. Our real work is in the groups we form through the people we draw in from the fair. After each fair, we run a small group with people we've met at the fair and elsewhere who are interested in knowing more about God. We then facilitate further encounters with God and try to draw them into community.

At this point we are strategising the next step with the people who have stuck around and who want more.

Perhaps the best way to preserve the presence of humility and love in the prophetic is to take it outside the church.

Occasionally, prophecy can become overly religious and weird in the church. It rarely does in a biker bar or at a New Age fair. Naturally, all of us would like to have an experience like the one I just described. I truly believe that we all can. We must, however, begin where we are right now and faithfully risk speaking out the revelations that we receive, general and incomplete as they are. My confidence rests, not in our ability to hear God, but in God's ability to speak to us and to share with us his wonderful heart of invitation. As Paul says, we can know what God is thinking (1 Corinthians 2:16); however limited, we can see what he sees.

WHERE TO START: GOD'S INVITATION

What is God's heart for us? Some think, as Jim did in the story cited at the beginning of this book, that he is like an angry grandfather who has too many children and is now frustrated because he can't control them. God is certainly not like that. "'For I know the plans I have for you,' says the Lord. 'They are plans for good and not for disaster, to give you a future and a hope'" (Jeremiah 29:11). God is not anxiously waiting for the opportunity to bring judgment. On the contrary, he is delaying judgment in order to let mercy finish its work. He is not willing that any should perish (2 Peter 3:9).

What kind of Father is he? We see his heart expressed in Jesus' meeting with the Samaritan woman (recorded in John 4). This was a person rejected on three counts: She was a half-breed from a race that the Jews had rejected, she was a woman in a male-dominated culture, and she was an outcast in her village because of a trail of ended relationships – out on three strikes![10] Yet Jesus saw something else. He saw and affirmed the amazing invitation of God to her. He saw her hunger for what is genuine and real, her hunger for God himself. He saw not what was but what could be. That was what he called forward in her.

This is the heart of God – this is God's way of seeing. God wants us to learn how to see through his eyes of invitation. Paul admits in 2 Corinthians 5:16 that he lost sight of that earlier in his life. In fact, he says, he was guilty of evaluating Jesus from an earthly perspective. It resulted in him actually opposing the very Son of God! Similarly, we need to be very careful about this. Human nature leads us to see competitively. We see what isn't in people in order to help us feel better about ourselves. Yet this is destructive for all of us: We continue to feel badly about ourselves *and* others while becoming increasingly isolated and separated from the comfort that relationship brings.

God has not given us a message of condemnation but a message of hope. We communicate that hope best by identifying the image of God in the person and inviting it forward.

---

[10]Some commentators see in the fact that she had had a series of husbands and was presently in a relationship with a man that was not her husband that she was likely viewed as a highly immoral woman. Others point out that it is possible that all her previous husbands had died or that she had been divorced by them because of some kind of disease. In that case, perhaps her present living arrangement was more of a working agreement than a sexual one – that no one dared to be husband number six! Whatever the circumstance, the end result was that she was considered taboo among her own people, simply adding to her experience of rejection.

TWO ESSENTIAL LENSES: HUMILITY AND LOVE

The greatest enemy of the prophetic is self-focus. When our eyes are on ourselves and the potential benefit we may receive from praying for or speaking to others, we are in a dangerous place. Sometimes this self-focus is the result of pride. Successful experiences of God using us through prophecy can lead to an unhealthy confidence in our revelatory gifts. Peter's early experiences with revelation (Matthew 16–17) ought to sober us, as should Paul's caution that all prophetic revelation in this life is and will be incomplete (1 Corinthians 13:12).

Paul encouraged the Philippian believers to keep their primary focus on others (Philippians 2:3–4). This advice has been of central importance to me in trying to grow as a prophetic person. Because of my lifelong struggle to earn acceptance by succeeding, I would naturally approach prayer opportunities consumed with thoughts such as: "How am I going to do? Will my revelation be accurate?" While coping with these fears, I would be combing the recesses of my mind, searching for what seemed to be promising revelatory material. When I allow this pattern of thinking to take place, the ministry time becomes all about me and I usually get stuck in a quagmire of uncertainty and self-doubt.

To avoid falling into that pattern, I now almost always begin by consciously laying down my fears and ambitions, while making myself available to be used by God in any way he wishes. I then intentionally pray, "God, how do you see this person? What is it that you want to call forward and encourage in them?" I don't try to be prophetic; I try to catch God's heart for them. I try to see them with the compassion and enthusiasm with which God sees them. Once I can catch that, I speak from it. I don't worry whether what I say is prophetic or not. Prophetic gifting isn't supposed to be self-conscious but other-conscious. When it succeeds in this, it invariably produces the best kind of result.

A PRACTICAL, PROPHETIC PRAYER MODEL

At this point, we should take a moment to explore how to apply practically everything that has been said so far to praying with individual people. How can we connect them with the wonderful kingdom invitation that exists in God's heart? When we "see" what God wants to do, how can we join our hands and voices to his?

John Wimber proposed an answer to this question. He studied the New Testament through this lens of enquiry: "How did Jesus and the first disciples pray?" As a result of that study, he suggested a five-step prayer model based on their approach. That framework has revolutionized the ability of people all over the world to pray in tune with the Holy Spirit's leading and activity.

John's approach rested generally on two foundational influences. The first was the theology of the kingdom which he encountered during his years lecturing at Fuller seminary. It was here that he was introduced to the writings of George E. Ladd and what is now quite widely referred to as inaugurated eschatology, i.e. that the powers of the coming age were already being inaugurated in Jesus, even while the present, evil age had not yet been brought to an end.

The second influence on his practical prayer model was more historical than theological. John came to Christ in a Quaker church and this tradition affected his expectation of experiencing the kingdom. The Society of Friends (the term they used to describe themselves – others derisively used the term "Quakers" to mock their physical response to the Holy Spirit's presence in their meetings) was formed by a man named George Fox in the seventeenth century. They had a strong belief in God's desire to reveal himself in very powerful ways in worship. As a result, they developed a "waiting" posture during their worship times, hoping for what they termed an "opening", when God's Spirit would powerfully come upon them.

This historical expectation was reinforced by John's experience of the Jesus People revival in California in the 1970s, where powerful encounters with God were the norm. The expectancy of signs and wonders meshed with the concept of kingdom breakthrough in kingdom theology to produce John's prayer and ministry model. The early Vineyard was marked by a listening, waiting posture – inviting the Spirit and then carefully trying to follow his presence and activity. While the preaching and teaching was usually centred on the kingdom message and designed to stir faith for the miraculous, during the resulting ministry times, people were often encouraged to "dial down" (i.e. calm their anxiety), the understanding being that it was just as easy to run past the Holy Spirit as it was to lag behind.

John's approach is the foundation of what I will suggest here, although I am going to simplify it to what is essentially a two-step model. I have never been good with approaches that involve multiple steps, e.g. seven steps to casting out any demon, eleven steps to ensuring that everyone will love you. I can usually remember the first two, but I live in constant fear that I'll somehow get stuck between steps four and five and, as a result, permanently injure my future well-being or, even worse, the destiny of another! Here are the two steps (almost as easy as left, right):

Listen

We must develop and maintain a constant posture of listening and watching. Continually focus your attention through questions like these: "Lord, what is your invitation here? What are you seeing/doing? What is it that you care about here?" This helps to remind us that the entire prayer process is to be dynamically led by the Holy Spirit, not executed by us on his behalf.

It is important that we listen on two levels: To the people we are praying for and to God's Spirit. We need to ask people what they want prayer for. There are a number of reasons for this. First, it gives us information about their situation that enables us to pray more specifically. (This assumes that none of us hears so completely from God that we know precisely how to pray from divine revelation alone. It helps us to know that even Jesus asked diagnostic questions. In Mark 9:21 we read that he asked the father of the boy who was having seizures: "How long has he been like this?")

Second, genuinely listening to the people we are praying for helps us to develop an "other-focus". One main impediment to praying effectively for others is our extreme self-focus. We are so concerned about ourselves and how we are going to do in our prayer time, that it is very difficult to access fully the compassion and faith that God wants us to have. Gifts don't flow easily when our eyes are facing inward. However, once we catch God's heart for the person, we tend to get caught up in his flow of mercy and it is much easier to stay in step with what God is desiring to do.

Last, truly listening to people can help us see early signs of God's work being established in them. We may detect faith emerging within them or see the presence of God's Spirit on them. This can greatly encourage our own faith.

As we listen to people, we need to be listening and watching for the Holy Spirit. This is reflected in a few different ways. First, as we are receiving information from the person to help determine what it is we need to pray for, we need to listen for God's diagnosis. Our human make-up is characterized by complex interrelationships between body, soul and spirit. What originates in one sphere inevitably affects the others; symptoms in one area may actually be a result of root problems in another.

This is illustrated in the New Testament. In Matthew 17, Jesus discerns by the Spirit that the cause of a young boy's seizures is actually demonic (as is the woman's back problem in Luke 13). In John 5, the cause of the man's physical situation seems to be connected to a pattern of sin. Yet in John 9, the man's physical blindness is unrelated to either sin or the demonic. In each circumstance, we need the divine insight of the Holy Spirit or we will err in one of two directions: We will fail to direct our prayers specifically to the root of the problem or we will begin to construct "rules" to explain these connections and run the danger of becoming like Job's friends.

Second, once we have a sense from the Spirit whether there are any other factors or causes related to the presenting problem, we need to invite the Spirit's presence on the person. The whole prayer process is one of invitation. We begin by standing with the person in need, together inviting

God to release his mercy and the power of his kingdom into their situation. This is not an invitation of passive resignation. The disciples' prayer: "May your kingdom come soon. May your will be done here on earth, just as it is in heaven" (Matthew 6:10) is a confident battle cry against Satan's evil plans, but it does focus us on God's desires and intentions so that we can hear his specific revelation and receive his gifts. When Peter prayed for Dorcas to be raised from the dead (Acts 9), he prayed to God before he was able to speak *from* him.

Finally, we watch for responses of God to our prayers, recognizing that God's works of healing and deliverance are often not instantaneous. Throughout the prayer process, it is important to continue asking both the person receiving prayer and God, "What is happening?" Getting ongoing information can help us to focus and adjust our prayers to keep them aligned with what God is doing.

Learn to look for signs of God's presence and manifestations of his power in the person's body as well as in yourself. Ask questions about these manifestations. The purpose of these questions is not so much to evaluate whether or not God is going to heal (he certainly can do so without any observable indications); instead it is to confirm and direct our prayers more specifically. In Luke 8, when a woman who had been haemorrhaging for twelve years touched Jesus' robe, both he and she felt a release of power. Look for the presence of tangible power: It can help both to release faith and to direct continued prayer. When Jesus prayed for a blind man in Mark 8, asking the man: "What do you see?" enabled him to recognize that a partial healing had taken place and focused a second prayer.

Sometimes when I am praying for physical conditions, I will note that the pain associated with the condition I am praying for "jumps" to another part of the person's body. When I am aware of that, I often begin to focus on the spiritual connection to that pain. Continued observation and interaction makes that possible.

Obey

All prayer must begin with invitation – asking God to intervene and bring his kingdom. Implicit to it is the question: "God, what do you want to say and do?" When Peter was asked to pray for the kind woman, Dorcas, who had already died, the first thing he did was to get on his knees and pray the prayer of invitation. When we do that, however, there is the distinct possibility that God may answer us. When he does, our part in this divine dance shifts from Listen to Obey.

The most notable thing that marks the prayers of Jesus and the disciples are their words from God: "See!" "Lazarus, come out!" "Get up, Tabitha!" These are prayers of faith, of command. When we believe that God has told us what he wants to do, faith is released at some level within us. When we are convinced that God has spoken to us, we can confidently speak to the condition and the evil plan connected to it. This can't be made into a system; there is a big difference between bravado and faith. Nor do we have to raise our voice (as though volume will help us convince anyone – God, the devil or ourselves). When God has spoken, the only way we will grow in faith to see his work realized is to take the risk of speaking out what we believe he has said.

In Jesus' encounter with the Samaritan woman in John 4, God gives him revelation about the woman's past. Sharing this revelation is an important key to her recognizing that his love for her includes a full understanding of who she is and what she has done. It opens her heart to receive fully his invitation of unconditional acceptance. When Jesus recognizes that the cause of a boy's seizures is a spirit, he speaks with authority from God and rebukes the spirit, commanding it to leave. With the confidence of knowing God's purposes for the situation, Jesus literally commands the dead man Lazarus to come out of his tomb (John 11). Indeed, Jesus told his disciples, nothing is beyond our reach if God has spoken and we have the courage to pronounce it (Matthew 21:18–22).

Many years ago, I experienced this gift of faith in the midst of a very trying circumstance. Our only child to survive pregnancy was a strapping two-pound boy we named Jonathan. Miraculously, he had lived in spite of the odds, a credit far more to the mercy of God than to any faith on my part. Since the birth of our son, Joy had suffered two miscarriages and was within an hour of losing yet another baby – we were becoming quite expert in the whole business of miscarriages. Consulting with the doctor only confirmed this fact. Finally (it was now in the middle of the night), I couldn't bear it any more and retired to another room, where I sadly began to pour out my anger toward God (Why do we always seem to treat our friends like our enemies?) because he had given us a number of promises for this little baby.

Surprisingly, in the middle of my self-justified tirade, God spoke to me from Scripture. In a sense, he simply asserted: "I said I would do it and I will." This word came with spiritual force, hitting me in the chest like a hammer. A deep sense of peace and certainty came over me. I knew that God had declared his intentions. Without any premeditation, I began to speak to the plans of the devil for ill and I rebuked them, literally commanding the miscarriage to stop. Some time after that I must have fallen asleep. All I know is that I woke with a start a few hours later, chiding myself for such lack of commitment and perseverance. I rushed into the next room to discover that God had stopped the miscarriage in its tracks. Our daughter Jaana is the delight of our lives today!

Not all faith comes to us in a fully mature expression. The reality, as Paul reminds us in 1 Corinthians 13:12, is that we hear imperfectly and cannot always be absolutely sure that what we think we have heard is unmistakably God. This uncertainty is what makes the quest for faith the journey that it is. Like Abraham and Sarah, we must step toward what we believe God has shown us, even though at times we have little idea where that is leading.

How do we grow in our ability to discern when God has really spoken and when it is just our imagination? The author of Hebrews suggests that a major aspect of growing in discernment has to do with taking what we believe is the good and right thing and acting on it. He describes the mature as those "who by constant use have trained themselves to distinguish good from evil" (Hebrews 5:14 NIV). The heroes of the faith (Hebrews 11) said and did what they heard. If we want to move beyond simply being legends in our own minds, we must do the same.

Once we believe God has spoken to us, we need to battle relentlessly for that promise to become reality. Double-mindedness is the enemy of faith. While it is helpful and important to evaluate the fruit of our hearing from God, if we do so too quickly, we will be paralyzed by indecision. The rule I follow is this: If I believe God has given me some direction, it will take a stronger, clearer "word" from God to cause me to question what I heard first.

Similarly, we ought not to be too quickly satisfied by signs of God's presence if they fall short of what we believe to be God's invitation, e.g. "They felt God's peace ... Some inner healing took place ... God gave them some reassuring promises." We must be relentless in pursuing all God might want to do, continuing to focus our prayers and, blessing what God is doing, asking more specifically for his kingdom to come. As Jesus' story of the persistent widow in Luke 18 illustrates, God is not an unjust judge but a kind, compassionate Father who loves to give good gifts to his children. Often the key issue in prayer lies in our lack of perseverance rather than God's unwillingness to give.

A few years ago I was training a large group of people in Canada in how to apply these principles practically. As they broke into teams for prayer, one of the teams gathered around a young woman who had come to the meeting on crutches, her right knee badly swollen. She could neither bear any weight on her right leg nor did she have any significant range of motion in the joint. When I came around to the group, they were quite pleased and ready to stop praying even though it was quite obvious to me that little had taken place with her injured knee. They were satisfied that she had experienced the touch of God's Spirit and an awareness of his love for her. Of course, this is wonderful (may we all have such an experience), but the revelation that had come in the meeting, that resulted in their praying for this woman, was that God wanted to bring healing to someone with a damaged right knee. As far as I could see, they were stopping well short of what God had invited them toward.

I began by encouraging them: Her experience of God's Spirit was a confirming sign that he indeed wanted to fulfil what he had promised. I asked them to focus their prayers and specifically ask God to release his healing presence into her right leg and knee to restore the joint completely. Over the next half an hour or so, I returned to the group at least three times, each time helping them to sharpen their prayers by blessing and acknowledging what God had done and further targeting their prayer on specific requests (e.g. bring relief to the swelling, restore flexibility to the joint). Finally, as their faith grew, I encouraged them to speak out what they believed God had promised to do, with the full expectation that it would take place. By the end of their prayer time, which had now continued at least thirty minutes beyond when they were first ready to stop, the young woman had discarded her crutches and was literally able to kick and jump with joy. Only by being relentless about fully realizing God's intention for the prayer time did they see it take place.

The very nature of this spiritual battle in prayer underscores the value of, whenever possible, having a team of people praying. This greatly increases the potential for a variety of spiritual gifts to be expressed and can definitely raise the level of faith brought to the process. While one may have a particular strength in receiving revelation, another will have great faith for a release of God's power, and so on.

Years ago I was praying in a team with one other young man. We were praying for a woman from another part of our country. She was quite nebulous about what it was that she wanted prayer for. I had a sense that the presenting problem was not the real issue, yet I simply could not uncover what it was. I worked very hard at doing so. Through questions, discussion and prayer, I kept probing and trying to connect her real place of need with God's Spirit. It was to no avail – this was a prayer time that was simply going nowhere.

What compounded the situation was that my team mate wasn't being much help. He didn't ask a question nor did he pray a prayer. In fact, he seemed quite disengaged, staring off into the distance. I had already determined that we would have a talk following this, where I would instruct him on the importance of "pulling one's weight", when he asked the woman one simple question, "Does the name Rebecca mean anything to you?" Immediately the woman broke into tears and began to share the discouragement and despair she felt about this relationship. The dam had broken and I repented. My friend's one brief contribution from God outweighed all the good things I had tried to do for God.

Whether praying as an individual or as a team, we reach a point when it is time to stop praying. How do we know we have reached that point? I believe there are three possible scenarios. First, the person may have been, as far as we can see, completely healed and/or delivered. In that case, we can celebrate together the goodness of God to them, though his Spirit may use that healing to allow us to encourage or instruct them in another area.

My son, Jon, was praying for a woman in her early twenties who was blind in one eye in St. Petersburg, Russia. After a relatively short time of prayer, her sight was completely restored. While that prayer time was over, it opened a wonderful opportunity to introduce her to Jesus – the

One who had healed her. What a delight it was to see God's Spirit fill her as she gave her life to him. We then gave her counsel on the importance of becoming part of a community of faith.

Second, the person's condition may have worsened while praying, making it hard to convince them that further prayer would be helpful or even desirable. I have learned to see this kind of reaction as a very positive sign – at least something is happening! An encounter of some kind is taking place and it can only be a matter of time before God breaks through.

I didn't always see it that way. Almost twenty years ago, my father had a tragic accident at the age of sixty-four. He fell out of a cherry tree from a considerable height (he had been picking cherries in the rain) and landed on his head. (If you understood my family, it would be perfectly clear to you why he was picking cherries in a wet tree.) As a result of his fall, he broke his back in three places.

At the time of the accident, I was just returning to my office after experiencing my first healing. I had prayed for a friend with a ruptured disk and, to my astonishment, he was able not only to get out of bed but touch his toes without pain. Just as I arrived, I got the call. Immediately I heard a demonic voice challenge me: "If you continue to try to do this, I will attack everyone you love." My heart sank.

When my father got to the hospital, the prognosis was not good. While he was not paralyzed, the doctor spoke of a very long recovery period due to his age and said categorically that he would never lift more than ten pounds again in his life. My father was in excruciating pain (this was the first time he had ever been in hospital) and my prayers weren't much help. In fact, I was so discouraged that the only prayers I could muster were the kind that barely escape your mouth, only to run down your chin and drop onto the floor. There was absolutely no result to my prayers. What had happened to the "man of power for this hour" that had so recently seen the kingdom come?

For three days, my father was in more and more pain and spoke constantly of dying. It seemed he had lost his will to live. On that third day, I was deeply agitated. A thought kept running through my mind: "Go and rebuke a spirit of death!" I kept dismissing it, confused as to what it meant and unsure of how I would actually go about doing it. ("Excuse me, Nurse, I have come to rebuke a spirit of death.") This was a little outside my comfort zone.

I was hounded by this thought all day long. By the end of the day, I knew I had to do something. Joy and I went to the hospital. Joy shared a word that she felt God had given her. I looked straight into my dad's eyes and said, "Dad, this is not your time to die. I'm calling you to life!" Joy and I, along with my mother, prayed for my dad with renewed enthusiasm and actually a little faith! While we prayed, my father heard a voice say to him, "Your back will be as good as or even better than it has ever been!"

What happened as a result of this step of obedience? Nothing … no, it was worse than nothing. For the rest of the day, my dad got appreciably worse. Any seed of faith that I had was stamped into the ground. From my perspective, all hope was gone.

When my father awoke the next morning, he was surprised; it was the first time he had slept in three days. The next thing he noticed was that he had no pain. This was followed immediately by the realization that he had no pain no matter what he did. Therefore he did what to him was the most natural thing: He got up and began to shave, getting ready to check himself out of the hospital.

The nurse who arrived in his room saw things from a different perspective, however, and soon a conference of sorts was taking place with various medical people and my dad. After a considerable amount of demonstration on my father's part and signing a waiver, he was allowed to return home.

The following day he went for a seven-mile walk (unfortunately without telling my mother, who was driving the streets looking for him) and within a week, he helped his brother do a renovation to his house. By the second week, he drove to the centre of Canada (a three-day drive), returning two weeks later. It was at that time that he checked into the doctor's office for further x-rays. They discovered that my father's back was still broken in three places! The doctor was unable to explain how my father was able to do what he had been doing. My dad's comment, "I guess having a broken back isn't all that bad if I can continue to do everything I ever did!"

A year later, my dad helped me with a major renovation to my home: Raising beams, wheeling cement and hauling bricks. After days of badly outworking me, he remarked with tears in his eyes, "My back is better than it ever was!" Since that time, I am quite encouraged when a person's condition quickly worsens with prayer. God could just be on the move!

A final possibility that indicates the prayer time may be over is when everyone has prayed everything that they can think to pray with absolutely no effect and God seems absent from the entire process. After a certain time of waiting, simply to see if there is any revelation that God wants to release or any signs of his presence and/or work to bless, it's time to leave our prayers in his hands. However, we must never say that nothing has happened. I have had so many experiences that have contradicted my early judgments: God can heal powerfully without any external indications.

Just a few months before John Wimber died, he and I prayed for a childless couple that had been unable to have children for quite a number of years. We had both seen our prayers for fruitfulness answered so many times that we were quite confident of God's goodness coming to them. That is, before they began to share the extent of their difficulty. Though I can't recall all the details, I know that each of them had medically verified reasons why they couldn't conceive (the wife had at least three major impediments to conception). At one point, we had to stop them sharing anything further so that we would still have enough faith to pray at all!

When we did so, even though the couple themselves seemed full of hope, literally nothing happened in the prayer time. There wasn't even a sense of God's presence in any of us. It was one of those prayers that you want to conclude with an apology. You can imagine my surprise when, about four years later, I met this couple while visiting their city. At first I didn't recognize them. I had never seen her pregnant and I had certainly not seen their two children. From their account, she conceived within a week or two of our prayer and now almost seemed to have a spiritual gift of conception! Don't be afraid to stop praying when there is nothing left to pray, but never say, "Nothing happened!"

READING THE WORDS, DOING THE WORKS

DISCUSS IT

In this chapter, Gary tells stories of some the unexpected tools of revelation that came during prayer times.

- Share a story about some of the tools you have used to see God's kingdom come in a prayer situation.

Are there other tools that you "earnestly desire"?

- Pray for each other.

Have you seen God's miracles come in the marketplace?

- Share to encourage each other.
- If not, ask God for situations this week and pray for each other.
- Keep your eyes open and go for it when an opportunity comes along.
- Check with each other next week and share your stories.

DO IT

Take Gary's two-step prayer model and unpack it.

- What are the ingredients or aspects of Step 1 (Listen) and Step 2 (Obey)?
- See if you can reduce all Gary says to a simple statement that you will always remember.

Purpose to pray for anyone God brings across your path.
- Try to focus on the person and not on your doubts and insecurities as you listen to God.
- If no opportunity comes this week, ask again next week.
- Continue until you see something happen in this regard.

PRAY ABOUT IT

Are you tempted to stop short when praying for people?
- Purpose to catch God's heart for the person you are praying for.
- As you pray in teams, share with the others what you are hearing so that the whole picture can become clearer and the gifts can help one another.

THINK ABOUT IT

Is the enemy holding you hostage by intimidating you as you pray for healing? Is he threatening you with penalties for your prayers? Face the threats and go straight towards the enemy just as David headed towards Goliath. Gary talked about his dad's healing. We may never have experienced this miracle if we hadn't faced the threat of death.

CHAPTER 4

EMPOWERED BY GOD'S SPIRIT

THE DIVINE MISSION

> For he has rescued us from the one who rules in the kingdom of darkness, and he has brought us into the kingdom of his dear Son. God has purchased our freedom with his blood and has forgiven all our sins. (Colossians 1:13–14)

The apostle Paul writes these reassuring words to the believers in Colosse in the context of a prayer encouraging them to be both patient and persevering. To borrow another of his encouragements (that given to the disciples in Philippi), they can work with confidence because God is truly at work in them.

We are all recipients of the divine mission of Jesus. He came from heaven both to rescue us from the powers of darkness and to reconcile us to a place of protection within God's love and care. This place, however, is right in the middle of the kingdom of these dark powers. That is because the full intention of God's love reaches beyond our own redemption. It has always been God's plan that those he rescues become his rescuers. He wants to capture our hearts so fully with his love that we become passionate about the things he cares passionately about. To follow Jesus, then, means eventually to go back with him to the spiritual dungeon from which we were freed – this time to reclaim the lives of others who have responded to his call to freedom and restoration.[1]

On the one hand, we can do this with great boldness because Satan's dungeon is no longer secure. Jesus "disarmed the evil rulers and authorities … on the cross" (Colossians 2:15). The door can no longer lock us out; Jesus has the keys! From Satan's perspective, no one is safe from God's divine reclamation. Knowing this, however, should not make us cocky or arrogant – Satan may be defeated, but he is filled with rage and ready to defend his prison with every means at his disposal.

The call to divine rescue is not a Sunday walk in the park. There is no "Welcome Rescuers!" sign to greet us.

---

[1] I do not want to leave the impression that God's goal is to take us out of the world rather than to transform it. If we are not careful, we can imply that our real home is heaven, not a renewed earth, and that we are here to get people into heaven, rather than to recruit them into the movement of which Jesus is the head and that will eventually see his kingdom realized here on this earth. As N.T. Wright insists, eschatology is this-worldly, i.e. our ultimate goal is ruling the world with Jesus, whether as resurrected or transformed (*The New Testament and the People of God*, Minneapolis: Fortress Press, 1992, pages 320–334, 460–462; also *What Saint Paul Really Said*, Grand Rapids: William B. Eerdmans, 1977, pages 140– 142.) Heaven is at best a "holding pen" that we would just as soon not need. Naturally, in a sense we are releasing people from Satan's power, but in another sense we are taking over the prison and transforming it into the paradise God intended it to be. Satan is the one who goes out, i.e. is cast out/cast down/bound in prison/tossed into the Lake of Fire.

Instead our task reads much like that of Moses walking into Pharaoh's court in the time of the Exodus. The first response in both settings is, "Don't even think about it! These people are staying right here." Christ's mission always involves power encounters.

Jesus was and is never intimidated by these encounters. In his earthly ministry, he was always fully united with his Father, the source of all power and authority. He never allowed anything to separate him from his Father's will. He trusted his Father in every way and obeyed him implicitly. As a result, the demons invariably tried to flee from his presence. They were no match for the power of God that backed Jesus' words and deeds.

We realize that potentially that same authority can be ours. Our difficulty lies in keeping our eyes fixed on Jesus, following his every step and obeying his every instruction. Like Peter trying to walk on the water, we find it difficult to stay focused on Jesus and ignore the threats coming from all directions. Instead, like Peter, our confidence and trust wavers and we soon become separated, disconnected and overwhelmed. Soon we are crying out for our own salvation!

OUR NEED FOR EMPOWERING

We realize that our weak, immature faith needs to be empowered with confidence and boldness – much like we see in the early church. When we examine the later Peter, during and following Pentecost, there is a marked difference in authority and courage. And he is not the only one! Though the early church had many problems, they seemed to be filled with an unshakeable confidence that God was with them and that, through the partnership they had with

God by his Spirit, they could do amazing things. They also had, early on, a deep sense of unity that enabled them to seek God together and trust him to do powerful things in and through them as a community (Acts 2:42–47).

How then can we discover the faith and power that they had? It would seem that Pentecost was a key turning point for the early church. Jesus clearly told them that something powerful and significant would take place: "When the Holy Spirit has come upon you, you will receive power and will tell people about me everywhere," he said (Acts 1:8).

EMPOWERING IN THE VINEYARD

One of John Wimber's primary contributions was to remind the evangelical church, of which he was fully a part, that the Great Commission (Matthew 28:18–20) we have all embraced is to be an empowered partnership. While this commission was always John's central focus, he thought it meant far more than faithful obedience on our part (although it meant that as well). The very Spirit of the Creator of heaven and earth actually lives inside us. How could we possibly expect to live in that reality and not experience it powerfully from time to time? To paraphrase John, we have expected far too little of the Spirit's presence with us; he wants to express his presence strongly in and through us.

With this understanding so central to John's thinking, it is not surprising that the language of empowering played a prominent role in the early days of the Vineyard movement. When I first attended Vineyard conferences in the early 1980s, it seemed like every session either made reference to or gave some opportunity for an empowering experience. (Actually, in general conversation, the more common theological term was being "zapped". This seemed to be the Vineyard equivalent for what more Pentecostal believers have called "the baptism of the Spirit".) I soon came to the conclusion that this was the central key to kingdom ministry, the one thing you didn't want to leave home without.

I always came to conferences with the great expectation that I too could be zapped and enter into a whole new kingdom reality – most likely this would launch me into effective kingdom service, not to mention kick-start my international ministry! Though, in retrospect, this was certainly not what John was trying to encourage, I and many others became quite obsessed with "getting the power". I would come to session after session eagerly and very quickly learned the acceptable pre-zapping routine. It only made sense that, if God was going to empower you or touch you or land on you in a powerful way, you had to get into the proper zapping position. That usually meant, "Head up, hands open, hold that position and then wait." In my case, it seemed to be, "Wait and wait and wait a little more and keep reminding yourself that good wine takes time." However, after a few conferences, I started thinking, "God doesn't seem to be noticing me."

This was a problem, because I was already a Vineyard pastor. I had a very vested interest; I needed to be able to do the works of Jesus! Vineyard pastors were supposedly fully empowered and prepared to raise the dead by noon each day. Yet I carried this secret – I had the job, but I had somehow missed the inaugural zapping that is supposed to come with it. I did bring this issue up with God, but he seemed to be focused elsewhere (perhaps the Middle East was flaring up again). As a result, I decided to help the process along just a bit. During ministry times for empowering, I tried to do the kind of things that attract prayer team members to come and pray for you. (It's hard to be zapped when no one even gets around to praying for you!) I tried various things: Swaying back and forth, trying to look somewhat enraptured with perhaps the odd trembling motion thrown in.

One particular experience comes to mind. I was in a workshop with about seventy people. The workshop teacher was well known as being highly "anointed". When there was an invitation for empowering prayer, I jumped right up as did almost everyone in the room. Thankfully, I had the distinct advantage of having arrived at the workshop early enough to have a second row seat and was able to secure a prime spot near the anointing.

The prayer soon came, "Holy Spirit, come; let the power of God come!" I began my usual cheerleading for God, "Come on, God, you can do it!" Before too long, I became impatient and started peeking. Where was the prayer team? I guess I wasn't swaying enough, because they would walk right by me. Behind me, I kept hearing the sound of people falling. The frequency of these sounds both encouraged and frustrated me. On the one hand, God was clearly on the move. (It sounded like a spiritual logging operation!) On the other hand, he definitely seemed to be missing me. After some time and considerable thumps on the floor, I started to panic. I took a peek around me: There were only two people standing in the whole room and I was one of them. My greatest fear was realized. "Oh no," I thought, "I *am* the Antichrist!"

Out of this experience (or, rather, lack of it), I really began to question: "What is this empowering that we see in the Book of Acts? What does it mean to be 'baptized in the

Spirit'? Is this essential in order to do the works of Jesus and receive spiritual gifting? Will this lift me up to an entirely new plane of spiritual power and discernment?" And probably my greatest question was: "Why isn't this happening to me?"

THE BAPTISM OF THE SPIRIT

What, then, was this "baptism" that Jesus spoke of (Acts 1:5 – "in just a few days you will be baptized with the Holy Spirit") and is it something that we can experience today? The Greek word *baptizo* was not a technical, religious term. It was commonly used in a variety of settings and, like all words, it had a range of meanings depending on the context in which it was used. Generally, it referred to immersing one object into another. One common usage of the term had to do with the dyeing of cloth. The cloth would be immersed ("baptized") into the dye, uniting inextricably with the dye to become a new combined entity. This same word was also used to describe the sinking of boats in a deluge. As a result of a fierce storm, the boat could be overwhelmed by the waves and irreversibly "baptized" into the sea – subsequently separating boat and sea could only be done with great difficulty.

Both New Testament writers, Luke and Paul, utilize this term as a metaphor to describe the Holy Spirit's work in us. But how are we to understand what they are trying to tell us, especially since their writings seem to be somewhat contradictory? Most of us already have a piecemeal fabric of answers. They are part of our embedded theology – those beliefs that we have absorbed in the course of our journey, gathered from a variety of sources. Generally, there are two stereotypical answers given for the "baptism of the Spirit" (with some variation within each). The first viewpoint centres on the preposition "in", i.e. the indwelling Spirit; the second focuses on the role of the Spirit "on" individuals.

The Spirit "in"

The key verse of the first group is 1 Corinthians 12:13: "But we have all been baptized into Christ's body by one Spirit, and we have all received the same Spirit." They use this verse to interpret what Jesus meant by the term "baptized with the Spirit". Paul makes it clear, they will remind us, that this baptism is a uniting with Christ so that we become part of his body by receiving the Spirit. They reinforce this interpretation from Galatians 3:27–29: The Spirit unites us with Christ, making us a single, unified body with God and with one another. When Jesus tells his followers to wait in Jerusalem until the Father sends what he has promised, he is pointing back, they will tell us, to the discussion he had with his disciples just before the cross (recorded in John 14–16, just a few pages before Acts 1). This is the promise of the indwelling Spirit who has been given to guide and direct us, the One whom the disciples received in John 20:22.

This, of course, fits magnificently with the understanding of baptism as the dyeing of cloth: We are baptized into Christ and by the power of the Spirit become one with him, never to be separated. For them, the "baptism of the Spirit" is, quite simply, the new covenant. It happens when we receive Christ.

The Spirit "on"

The second group would not deny these verses or this reality. They would protest, however, "You just forgot a major part of the Bible. Read the Book of Acts!" They will point us back to Luke's writing in Acts 1 and 2 and on throughout the Book, drawing attention to the many and varied ways that the Spirit is described as coming "upon" people. They will emphasize the strong and seemingly intentional parallelism between Luke's Gospel and Acts (i.e. in the same way the Spirit came upon Jesus and others, he is now coming upon the church) and they will relate both back to strikingly similar language in the Greek Old Testament. In every major period of Israel's history, they will tell us, God's Spirit "came upon" them in powerful ways with powerful effect.

Jesus' words, quoted by Luke in Acts 1:4, properly relate to Luke 24:49, not John's Gospel, as this group would rightly say. Luke's expression in 24:49, "fills you with power", is the same expression as the Old Testament description of Gideon's empowering. And the first chapter of Acts naturally leads into the rest of the Book: The Spirit fills the believers and comes upon them in power, which results in explosive, prophetic (in the widest sense of the word) activity. Clearly, the "baptism of the Spirit" for Luke means the restoration of the Spirit of prophecy (notice Peter connecting the events at Pentecost with the prophet Joel in Acts 2:16), whereby the voice and presence of God, greatly diminished since the Exile in 586 BC, has been renewed within Israel.

What was poured out on Pentecost was the potential for everyone to receive this anointing of power that was reserved for the few in Old Testament times. Generally, they see this as an overwhelming experience or anointing of the Spirit that comes subsequent to conversion/initiation – often referring to conversion as the receiving of the Spirit and the "baptism of the Spirit" as being "filled with the Spirit" with new power. This is a "baptism," like a deluge that overwhelms our "boats" with unmistakeable force and power.

This is the language of anointing, they would stress; it is a releasing of the Spirit's power that enables us to live on a new plane of spiritual victory and power.[2] They support their interpretation with amazing stories. ("Before I received 'the baptism', I was a 112-pound spiritual weakling; now I am a 250-pound giant throwing demons out of every window.") Amazingly, many of these stories are true. The fastest growing segment of Christianity today is the Pentecostal/ charismatic segment. It has propelled Christianity forward around the world. This expansion has been marked by experience with power.

How can you know that you have had this experience? The defining mark for many within this group is the gift of tongues, similar to what was experienced at Pentecost. Others look for signs of prophetic activity that demonstrates that "you got it". Whichever the acceptable sign, the fact remains that this is seen as a second tier of Christian experience that is crucial for sanctification and service.

---

[2]The concept of "anointing" is a familiar one in the Old Testament (where it denotes the setting apart of kings and prophets), but it is not strongly carried over into the New. Where it is referenced, it is done in a way that is quite different from the way popular preachers speak about it today. Peter makes the point in his first letter (chapter 2) that we have all been anointed as God's holy priests. John refers to "the anointing" as the Holy Spirit, whom we have all received. He makes the point that he teaches us all the truths of God, so that we don't need to rely on a gifted few. This, of course, is not to ignore those in the New Testament and church history, such as Paul, who seem to be specially gifted or "anointed" by the Spirit. We might fairly question, however, the exact nature of this giftedness. Is the measure of God's Spirit flowing through Paul's life a special "anointing" from God or is it a simple result of his zeal to respond to his powerful spiritual encounters with radical, uncompromising obedience?

Strengths and Weaknesses

Each of these perspectives has great strengths but also some weaknesses. The strength of the first is most likely theological. In my view, they certainly understand this issue of person versus power and the dangerously Gnostic tendencies in seeking after anointing. For the first group, this talk of a second experience or anointing comes dangerously close to treating the Holy Spirit as a power rather than a person. We don't receive his big toe the first time, his elbow the second and his right ear lobe the third time so that if we get enough baptisms, we will eventually get the whole person. We get the Spirit upon conversion – all of him. Anyone who doesn't have the Spirit of Christ doesn't have Christ, they say, agreeing with Paul (Romans 8:9). The key issue in empowered living cannot be receiving more of the Holy Spirit; it has to do with him receiving more of us as we surrender to his Lordship.

Sadly, however, sometimes this theological strength has not been used to enhance our continuing experience of the Spirit, but has served to restrict it. As John Wimber described it, "Sometimes good labels mask poor medicine!" In the church where I grew up, I learned very quickly that prophecy today is to be understood as the Sunday sermon. (I used to think, "Prophecy is really hurting!") What is healing? Healing is doctors. What about deliverance? Actually, we didn't talk about deliverance. And we certainly didn't seek tongues (which wasn't a major problem, because we never talked about this gift in any setting, which made it appear rather clandestine!).

The theological labels haven't always been the best in the second group, although much of the experience has been life changing. That is not to say that this more charismatic group has not been guilty of an exaggerated dualism – setting up a straw man and then knocking it down: "All was marked by sin, doubt and weakness in my evangelical drudgery. Then I experienced the baptism of the Holy Spirit. Since then it has been nothing but unrelenting faith, power and victory!"

The reality tends to be somewhat different. Certainly there are wonderful, incredible stories of people having visitations of the Spirit that are experienced like liquid love flowing down from heaven. Our own son-in-law had such an experience in his earlier life in the middle of an acid trip (he describes it as being like ten thousand volts of electric love coming from God). Not only was he immediately "straight", but it completely changed the course of his life. Since that time, he has wholeheartedly pursued God's plans for him. Yet, at the same time, there are other people who have sought this kind of experience, but instead find themselves pacing in their bedroom practising "ShouldaBoughta-Honda."[3] What do we do with that? Some of the "unrelenting life of faith, victory and power" that is advertised manages

---

[3]This identifies one of the continuing difficulties that classical Pentecostal believers have: The frustration of good people not "getting" an experience of the Holy Spirit evidenced by speaking in tongues. As Brent Cantelon, a Pentecostal pastor and good friend, has helpfully reminded me, often people can be helped through that frustration and blockage in receiving this gift of speaking in tongues by recognizing that, while the Holy Spirit is not limited, our ability to release and communicate without encumbrance is. Faithfully using whatever expression we believe the Spirit has given us, however simple and uncomplicated, can prime the pump, so to speak, for a greater fluidity. Nevertheless, the fact remains that some wrestle for years with the nagging sense that they are simply repeating phrases they have made up.

to bypass a fair amount of holiness or character. What kind of faith, power and victory is that?

What we desire is the best of both these worlds. We want the expectation, faith and experience, which is the strength of the second group, along with the protection and wisdom of the first group's good theology (not to mention, character in both!). We want to be freed from the kind of pressure I described earlier of having to have some kind of personal defining experience that will rewire our whole inner nature. Yet we want to rise above the kind of Christian discipleship that has little or no hint of the miraculous but seems to be largely self-effort (God playing a relatively invisible role, supplying grace from a distance).

GOOD MEDICINE, GOOD LABELS

To that end, let's revisit the context of Jesus' words in Acts 1. For almost six hundred years, God's chosen people had been living in a state of expectation and longing. The prophecies of Isaiah and Jeremiah had never been fulfilled, which deepened the sense that they were still in Exile. The Spirit of prophecy, the prophetic voice of God throughout their history that helped to define them as a people different from all other people on the face of the earth, had not been entirely absent (prophets were never that common in Israel's history), but neither had the prophecies been fulfilled. For a people who saw themselves as the people of God's presence (Exodus 33:12–23), led by the voice of God to them through their kings and prophets, this was a disturbing time. God seemed to have forgotten them, never forgiving their sins or allowing them to return from Exile (in that they were subject to the

Romans). Prophets had arisen only to be crushed. Yet increasingly there was a stirring of expectation – many voices were reflecting on the prophets' promises of the coming age and (in some interpretations) the Messiah who would usher it in. In contrast with the present oppression, hope was growing that God would speak and if necessary act again.

For the disciples, the issue was different. The Prophetic Voice had come. Jesus, the Son of God, had walked with them for three years and had not only talked with them but also, as a classic "leadership prophet", guided and directed them. They had seen the kingdom of God expressed through Jesus and had participated in it along with him. He too was executed, but unlike the other prophetic voices, he had been vindicated by the resurrection and now he ruled with undying life. But now they had a different dilemma. Jesus was repeating what he had told them prior to his resurrection: He was going to leave them and the Spirit was going to take his place. His encouragement was that this Spirit would literally live within them (he himself released the Holy Spirit to them when he breathed upon them – John 20:21). While temporarily removed from them, he would continue to intercede for them from his position at the right hand of the Father.

They no doubt had some uncertainty: "We know that this thing worked with Jesus in the flesh, when he was here holding our hands and directing us, commissioning us and explaining to us how to walk out this whole mission, but can it work with the Spirit?" When Pentecost came, what did they realize? They recognized that the Spirit that came into them with Jesus' breath was indeed the Spirit of prophecy that energized the prophets. The prayer of Moses

(Numbers 11:29), echoed in the promise of God through Joel (Joel 2:28–29), was being fulfilled before their eyes. This confirmed what Jesus was saying to the disciples (John 14:16–21): They would not need to hear from God through another messenger (even Jesus in the flesh); God's Presence would live within them! And not just them. "Now," prophesied Peter, quoting from Joel, "anyone who calls on the name of the Lord will be saved" (Acts 2:21).

ONE SPIRIT, TWO INTENTIONS

Who was this person that had both indwelt them and come upon them? The person of the Holy Spirit, the third member of the Trinity (as the church would come to describe him two centuries later as it reflected on its experience). Luke and John in their respective Gospels and later Paul in his letters all refer to the same Holy Spirit in their writings. The Holy Spirit is the inner counsellor that the disciples received when Jesus breathed on them, the common lifeblood that spiritually united them to Christ and to one another and the fire from God that filled them with courage and boldness at Pentecost. Each of these accounts is simply describing the same Spirit from a different "functional" perspective.

Let me illustrate what I am saying. Imagine that I came to work for you, hired because of my international reputation as a chef. Perhaps our relationship works perfectly for some time – we are both happy as I have a good work environment and you are eating better than you have for years. Then one day, you arrive home to discover two of the walls of your home are missing. When you run to me to discover what could possibly have gone wrong, I respond, "Didn't you know? I am not only a world-renowned culinary expert, I am a carpenter on the side – I am renovating your home!" What would your response be? Other than calling the police, it may sound something like this, "I'm sorry, but I invited you as a chef. I never asked you to renovate my house."

This is part of our problem with the Holy Spirit. Many have only invited him as counsellor and friend. He is that, of course, but he is more than that. He not only wants to nourish and guide us and unite us to the love of the Father, he also wants to overwhelm our boats, inflaming our hearts with vision, passion and courage. Both of these are different "baptisms" of the same Spirit.

A PERSON, NOT A POWER

What then is the Holy Spirit's relationship with power? Jesus told the disciples that they could expect a powerful encounter when the Holy Spirit came upon them. What is the nature of that power? This is very important in a spiritual age like ours in which there is a lust for power because of our great insecurity. What is the power? Are we seeking a person or are we seeking a power?

Is the promise of Acts 1:8 some kind of power charge? Is its effect something like taking a hair dryer wired for 110 volts and plugging it into a 220 socket – or, better yet, a 440 socket? Is this the power of Pentecost? Christianity on steroids? Is it an experience or "anointing" where we get our finger into the Holy Spirit socket and (Zap!) it rewires us so that we are now programmed for triumphant living? Is that what it is? If so, heaven help us all, because we will be the most dangerous people on the face of the earth. It stands in the face of almost everything the Word of God says about power.

I am convinced that the power these early believers experienced at Pentecost was an intense experience of the Person of the Holy Spirit who lived within them. This indwelling Spirit came upon them for a second, linked purpose, to propel them into mission. The intensity of that experience convinced them that the Spirit of Christ living in them was just as powerful and effective as Jesus walking beside them in the flesh. As a result, they were filled with boldness and courage. "If God is in us and for us in this way, who on earth could possibly stand against us?"[4]

In the confidence of that presence, they began to walk out the mission that was given them. At just the right times along the way, at critical times, they continued to have these sovereign experiences when the Spirit of Christ that was in them came upon them in power. This was the key to their courage – they were not alone, God was truly with them. Their faith expanded. With great faith usually comes great grace!

---

[4]One might ask, "Are you saying that there is nothing that is residual in these experiences, simply elevated faith that acts like a welcome mat for gifts of grace from God? Certainly, there seem to be many people who appear very 'anointed' and able to do very powerful things – even when they have many character failings and seem to be quite separated from intimate relationship with God." To some extent, this is a mystery in Scripture and you would have to argue from silence. I can say, however, that at the very least our singular focus should be on the person of the Holy Spirit and on our submitted relationship to him. As I will discuss later, any focus or attention on power is inherently dangerous. The line between actively desiring the Spirit to work powerfully through us and practising magic is a fine one.

A COMMUNITY, NOT AN INDIVIDUAL

We often underestimate the power of individualism in our modern, Western cultures. At our worst, we are entirely self-absorbed – almost to the point of imploding into our own navels. At best, we suffer a great loss of synergy by not recognizing the power of real community. While there can be some positive benefits (i.e. "though none go with me, still I will follow"), unless this individualism is redeemed, it can have very negative implications in our seeking the Spirit and his empowering.

We have largely lost the sense of "us" in Scripture. When we read the word "you", we almost always interpret it as singular. We have a less than mature understanding of our identity as the people or community of God. We define our spirituality almost entirely in individualistic terms. This perspective, when applied to the "baptism of the Spirit", can badly skew the Spirit's intended result.

Too often we have made Spirit baptism all about us and our personal validation. When that is the case, if we don't get a personal visitation from God, we feel abandoned. When God comes near us and we feel his power, we are on top of the world. When he seems far away, we are overcome by a sense of hopelessness. Even worse, we begin to compete with one another for the Holy Spirit's attention, as though other believers are our competition. We grasp at anointing, the power to achieve and to be significant within the Christian community. What a sad thing that must be for the Spirit, whose main intention is to unite us to Christ and to one another.

When we remember that it is a person we are seeking, not a power, and that we are one people, one body, we can truly celebrate God's visitation – no matter who experiences his presence! This is the key to empowering: The community prayer, "God empower us; fill us with courage and boldness. Let us know that you are alive and powerfully with us!"

What if we brought this perspective back into the illustration of my first empowering ministry times in the Vineyard? What if I had not assumed that we were all separate individuals scrambling for a limited provision from God – a kind of spiritual survival of the fittest? Instead of walking out of the room devastated because God was not within my reach and therefore most likely I would be on my own trying to do kingdom works, I could have been greatly encouraged: God had visited that room! He was not far away. The same God who so generously touched a majority of the people in the room could be counted on to be powerfully with us all outside that room. That perspective would have allowed me to celebrate what was taking place and perhaps join with what he was doing by blessing his touch on others. If anyone in that room was strengthened, we were all made stronger. Maybe next time the tables would be turned and they would be praying for me! Very likely that could be true.

I truly believe this is one of the reasons that movements see a diminishing of the Spirit's presence and power over time: We grieve the Spirit by fighting over him and approaching him as a means to an end. We scrap for increased "market share" of his available power without recognizing how much that wounds him as a person. (I have a recurring picture of the Holy Spirit wanting to come and visit the gatherings of his people, but as he comes near, he is deeply grieved. What he hears sounds just like the *Finding Nemo* movie: "Mine! Mine! Mine!") It is his presence in us as a united community that we need. That presence is what fills us with the courage that makes the church an unstoppable force – nothing else!

THE SPIRIT'S PRESENCE TODAY

The experience of the Spirit at Pentecost had a profound effect. The lives of those impacted seemed to be transformed. They went from a small band cowering in an upper room to fearless ambassadors for the kingdom. However, this experience seemed to be just one of many recorded in the Book of Acts. Apparently it was a normal occurrence for the Spirit to visit God's people and powerfully fill them with renewed courage and boldness.

Early in the life of this new church community, opposition came from both religious and political rulers, along with the spiritual intimidation of the demonic powers behind them (Acts 4). Peter and John were threatened and flogged and commanded to abandon their witness of Jesus. As they returned and shared this with the larger community, they immediately went to prayer, appealing to God for his intervention. This was no insignificant threat!

What did they pray? After affirming God's sovereignty and authority over every circumstance, they simply brought this circumstance to him. "Sovereign Lord," they cried, "show us that you are with us, that you won't leave us so that we can be empowered with courage and boldness to continue to obey fully what you have commissioned us to do!" They asked God to deal with this opposition on a spiritual level and overrule it, bringing a display of signs and wonders and healing power.

How did God respond? He so powerfully filled them with his presence that the room they were in literally shook. The disciples got the message: "The Spirit of God in us is just as powerful as when Jesus was with us." After that, Luke simply reports: "They preached God's message with boldness" (Acts 4:31), both in their words and their deeds.[5] As they did so, God authorized their obedience with an incredible display of his power. Throughout the early history of the church, we see repeated instances of these kinds of experiences, where the church's faith and confidence was renewed and their mission invigorated as God powerfully reminded them of his continued presence.

Do we need those kinds of reminders today? Or is our reception of the Spirit at conversion sufficient? I suspect that we are not any different from the first believers. The challenges of Satan's opposition pull our eyes away from faith to fear and unbelief. We need powerful reminders of the Spirit's power and potential to work through us – our faith infused with the recognition, "God is really with us, who can stand against us?"

D.L. Moody, the notable American evangelist of the last century, was asked why he kept speaking of and seeking the filling of the Holy Spirit. He reflected for a moment

---

[5] I agree strongly with Brent Cantelon's comment to me: "By far the greatest need today is the Holy Spirit's transformation that causes our hearts to love souls enough to try – with all our strength and with all of his available and promised power – to bring people to Jesus. Our land is desperately Godless and has lost its way; people die every moment, far from God. We must have the Holy Spirit's power and enabling! Arrogantly holding a position on the Spirit, whether 'in' or 'on', while the lost perish all around, is pharisaical."

and replied, "I suppose I leak." Is that not true of us all? God has visited us in the past and we said, "God, I will never forget you. I will never forget that I can trust you and rely on you." How quickly we forget! It is because of this weakness in our faith, individually and collectively, that we need repeated visitations of God's Spirit.

"Be sure of this," Jesus said, "I am with you always, even to the end of the age" (Matthew 28:20). God seems to delight in meeting us in our weakness, demonstrating his commitment to do this. He isn't frustrated by our need for reassurance. He is an affirming Father, who is pleased to remind us of his faithfulness and provision. When we reach for the empowering of God's Spirit together, we can be confident that these prayers are among those God loves to hear.

Let this be our constant prayer together: "Oh God, will you show us that you are the same yesterday, today and forever. Would you show us that your Spirit in us is just as powerful and mighty as in the days when you walked on this earth? Would you encourage our faith, just like you did for the early church? Would you come and touch us? Would you blow out a few of our walls, renovate a few of our rooms? Come, oh Lord, and cook us up a feast. We will eat it together and rejoice that you are here!"

READING THE WORDS, DOING THE WORKS

DO IT

All the seemingly great men and women of "power for the hour" that Gary talks about started by just doing the works. That is all we are going to do in our study time this week.

- If you are in a large group, divide into smaller groups of six or seven people.

- Invite the Spirit together and then listen for one or several people that he indicates he would like to touch today. Begin by just observing whom the Spirit seems to be visiting.

- Once you've identified a person (or persons), try to listen to what God may be saying about the person, prophetic invitations to pray over the person, etc. Work together in the group to discern common themes the Lord seems to be highlighting, using the insights he gives through each person.

- Take your time. Pray everything you believe the Lord is giving you for the person. He will work very creatively. The bit we may want to throw out or think is insignificant or off the wall may be the very thing that really touches the person's heart.

- Don't force anything down someone's throat. Check to see if the things that are prayed/spoken over the person have any significance or are meaningful to them. Don't worry if what you think you heard seems to be wrong. This is a learning process. There are bound to be some glitches or things that don't seem to "land" at the time. (Sometimes things become significant later.)
- Be as grateful for anyone the Lord touches or anything he does as if he has done it for you. We are a community; when one benefits, we all share the blessing. Learn to celebrate others' joy as your own!

CHAPTER 5

BRINGING THE KINGDOM TO PEOPLE

WHAT ARE WE CALLED TO DO?

I love to watch movies that fall into the historical fiction genre. (I add "fiction" because I recognize that most of what purports to be historical is at best revisionist history.) I suppose I like them because, in their compression of events that lasted years into a few cinematic moments, they convey such a sense of grandeur, intense focus and passion – especially the battle scenes! At one point in the movie *Braveheart*, two armies race toward one another and collide in complete, wholehearted commitment to their respective causes. While terrifyingly brutal, such a scene calls forth deep desires to capture that kind of dedication in my own life.

One principle that relates to our present kingdom task becomes clear in these battle scenes. In the midst of the bedlam that defines hand-to-hand combat, it is difficult to get an overall sense of the battle. Strategy is generally confined to the job at hand – defend, thrust, parry and so forth. The battle is so immediate and close (and disorienting), that there is no time or space to think of anything else. To use another familiar metaphor, in such a battle it is easy to lose the wood for the trees. When that happens, we become confused and begin to channel our energies and passions into directions that aren't helpful to our cause (as in the case of "friendly fire" in more modern warfare).

Our mission of extending God's kingdom is very much like this. It is a matter of life and death – ours and others'! This battle between light and darkness is also very intense and demands that we learn a number of ministry skills and spiritual disciplines. Yet we must not learn so much, so fast or engage so intently that we forget the essence of kingdom ministry. Certainly in our earlier stages, the most important thing we can hold onto is a clear, contextual understanding of what it is we are trying to do in an overall sense. There is much more to learn – important insights to mine and valuable skills and gifts to explore and unpack. Yet I am convinced that if we can hold a clear understanding of our mission in a holistic sense, we will be amazed at how God's Spirit will guide us creatively in walking out the journey practically.

John Wimber tells a story of an instance early in his attempts to walk out the ministry of Jesus practically. He had been praying for someone to be delivered from the influence of evil spirits that had plagued his life for some time. At first he felt quite overwhelmed, lacking confidence because of limited understanding, experience and skills. It seemed to John that the demons were quite secure in their ability to hold their ground. At one point, a spirit said to John, "You don't know what you're doing!" (A point with which John sadly concurred.) Then, however, the spirit overstepped itself. "And you don't have any authority." This snapped John out of his intimidated retreat. "I may not know what I'm doing," he thought, "but I know that this is what I'm authorized to do and I'm going to do it!" Shortly after that, the demons beat their retreat. John's focus was restored along with his confidence in God's ability to empower his simple obedience.

The lesson he learned was simple and straightforward: The most important weapon we have in battling our spiritual enemy is not a proven collection of how-to's, but a firm grasp of what it is we have been called and authorized to do. If we keep that in view, we can count on the Holy Spirit to direct our obedience.

At this point in our discussion of kingdom engagement, let's draw back from the fray to catch a bird's-eye view of the cosmic conflict that has existed between God and Satan throughout most of human history. In particular, let's attempt to see clearly our unique part in this conflict and how we can best join God in his work in strategically helpful ways. In Chapter 1 we looked at Jesus' announcement that he had come to bring Good News. We also saw how each of us has been called to the same ministry as Jesus. It is crucial that we keep central and crystal clear our understanding of what that Good News was and is.

THE GOOD NEWS OF THE KINGDOM

When Jesus began to read the scroll (unrolled to Isaiah 61) in the synagogue at Nazareth, he was deliberately explaining the purpose and significance of all he had done so far. "The Spirit of the Lord is upon me," he said, "for he has appointed me to preach Good News to the poor. He has sent me to proclaim that captives will be released, that the blind will see, that the downtrodden will be freed from their oppressors and that the time of the Lord's favour has come" (Luke 4:18–19). Many would have seen in his quotation of Isaiah a reference to the practice of Jubilee, the celebration of the fiftieth year, when ancestral land was returned, debts were forgiven and Hebrew slaves were released (Leviticus 25: 8–55; Deuteronomy 15:1–18, though there is no evidence of Israel actually observing this practice after the establishment of the monarchy, if at all).[1] The Jubilee was not a dead letter for many Jews of Jesus' day. In fact, a whole book was dedicated to telling the history of Israel according to the Jubilee principle (*Jubilees*). Because this hope of Jubilee had not died, there was considerable longing and expectation for some type of final Jubilee, the coming of the kingdom of a new age, bringing complete liberation from evil (including the forgiveness of the sins of the nation) and all its consequential bondage and oppression. According to his words in Nazareth, that is exactly what Jesus came to do.

As Paul later described in Colossians 1:13–14, Jesus came for the explicit purpose of rescuing us, his created ones, from our oppression and slavery in a dark, evil kingdom. He purchased our freedom through his own sacrifice, bringing us into the wonderful new age, where his will for us is accomplished. Paul similarly outlines this mission of Jesus in Ephesians 1:9–10: He came to fulfil the wonderful plan of God for us, established before the creation of world, a plan for reconciliation, bringing together everything that had been fragmented and separated from him through Jesus.

---

[1]This position was popularized by John Howard Yoder, *The Politics of Jesus* (Grand Rapids: William B. Eerdmans, 1994), pages 21–79.

Note that people are at the centre of all this activity. While Jesus' coming was Good News to the whole created but fallen universe, his primary ministry was to bring the healing that results from God's rule – an intention distinctly different from a mission devoted to fixing problems. The wording in Isaiah's prophecy is significant: Jesus came to comfort the poor, free the prisoners, heal the blind and release the oppressed. He did not devote himself in a detached way to the problems of poverty, bondage, disease and oppression. In the same way, we must take care to recognize that the central focus of our ministry is to bring the Good News of God's kingdom to the lives of people rather than treating specific, isolated problems.

The mission of Jesus, one that has been given to us, is to bring real people along a journey of freedom leading to restoration with the One who made them. Kingdom ministry is coworking with God to bring people together: Within themselves, with one another and with God their Creator. (In addition, by bringing them back under the authority of their Creator, creation is restored to the authority of human beings.)

THE FALL FROM GRACE

The world to which God sent his Son was not as he had created it. When we are introduced to God's first creation in the garden (Genesis 2), the picture is marked by complete freedom yet security. Under God's just rule, there is order and ample provision. Everything is bathed in love, joy and peace in an environment of complete unity and integration. Though there may already have been a major rebellion in the heavens involving Satan and a number of angels (Revelation 12:9),[2] originally humankind was safely protected from Satan's power through their relationship with and obedience to God (i.e. they were secure under God's authority – a concept we will discuss later).

Through a single act of disobedience, resulting from Satan's deception (Genesis 3), the first man and woman chose independence[3] without anticipating that their right to appeal to God's protection would thereby be blocked. As a result, they fell under the worst kind of bondage – one that effectively brought a curse to the entire created universe. The impact was immediate and cataclysmic: For the first time, they experienced separation from the life-giving presence and protection of God on every level. In its place, sin took root with all its resulting confusion and disintegration. This multiplying effect of sin was so pronounced that within a few chapters, God had to destroy most of humankind to slow its spread.

By the time of Jesus' coming, even the chosen people of God were oppressed – not just politically; they were also physically, relationally and spiritually broken. There was an abundance of relatively orthodox religious activity, but little

---

[2]The idea of rebellion in heaven is only clearly addressed in intertestamental literature and the New Testament. Scholars debate how this fits with the Old Testament narrative, especially since the New Testament itself is not clear about the timing.

[3]The original sin is said to be choosing to "know good and evil", i.e. to become judges and thus to replace God as the sole judge. That this was the intention is evident in the claim that they would "become like God". This action, then, is a declaration of independence, in essence a rebellion against God, which is repeated every time we judge one another.

authentic relationship with God himself, a condition that the New Testament identified in how few people recognized the intervention of God in Jesus. They were truly a lost people or, as Jesus described their situation, using metaphors they could understand, sheep without a shepherd. We are no less so today.

How does such a tragic fall from grace occur? We have alluded to a decisive encounter in the original garden between the first humans and a serpent (Genesis 3), but it will be helpful to examine it further within the larger context of the battle between God and Satan – one in which we are very much involved.

The Scriptures clearly portray one central fact: God is King over all. His supremacy is never in doubt. He was already here when everything that is, came into being (Genesis 1:1). Through him, everything was created and it only continues to exist because he gives it life and breath. "He existed before everything else began," is the way Paul describes it in Colossians 1:17, "and he holds all creation together." We need never worry for God. He isn't anxious. Even in these dark, last days, the Trinity isn't huddled up in heaven writing and rewriting new plans to recapture momentum and regain the upper hand in their conflict with Satan so that the end of the age can truly come. The devil can only resist God because God gives him the very life to do so; when God decides he is done … he is done! Luther was right: Satan is God's devil.

Yet God has allowed rebellion against his kingship. Why and how could this be so? To some degree, we are simply not given this information other than being assured that we will eventually see and understand the wisdom of God in this.

Authors such as C.S. Lewis may be right in their explanation that a universe that is characterized by love and freedom must make room for this eventuality;[4] but even this observation is a helpful insight rather than a watertight apologetic.

The leader in this rebellion, Satan, is progressively revealed as God's adversary. At first his role is not clearly revealed (perhaps because God was trying to convince Israel that there was only one of God and because Satan then, as now, hides behind cultural structures, governments and religions). The first detailed information about Satan comes in the later parts of the Old Testament and is developed in the Jewish intertestamental literature. It is the coming of Jesus, however, that seems to expose him and his role most clearly.

Though much about the original rebellion, Satan's background and the nature of his forces is not clearly explained, what is clear is his general strategy and goal – unable to strike directly at God, he is devoted to destroying the unity of God's creation by separating it from his protection and provision. It is not surprising, then, that the primary focus of his destructive energies would be on human beings, those made in God's image. As early as Genesis 3, we find

---

[4]C.S. Lewis, *The Problem of Pain* (San Francisco: Harper SanFrancisco, 2001). This is part of the answer to the problem of evil: Why would a good God who knows the future allow sin to enter his world? The answer is that "love" which is forced, which does not have the opportunity not to love, is really not love at all. True love is the choice to love. Likewise the person who is "beaten into submission" or manipulated into submission is not really submitted at all, for they have no other choice. For there to be true love and obedience, there must be the possibility of choosing not to love and obey. Because of this freedom of choice, it is also possible for them to choose truly to do it.

him employing the basic strategy that he will use repeatedly throughout the history of humankind.

As we read this account, it is important to identify what didn't happen. There wasn't a supernatural "raiding party" that fought their way into the garden, overpowering the guarding angels, while Satan made a grab for the humans. Instead, God apparently allowed[5] the encounter between the first humans and Satan because a kingdom characterized by love and voluntary submission must allow temptation (the presentation of an alternative to loving and submitting to God) for choice to be truly free.

In the abridged description of the conversation that takes place between the serpent and the woman, we see the devil executing his plan for eventual domination and destruction. (For men hoping to beg off at this point, it is important to note that the text says that Adam was with her rather than conscientiously working somewhere else in the garden.) There are three elements to Satan's plan that have become his trademark through the ages.

Satan and Deception

First, Satan attempts to deceive. "Did God really say …?" he asks the man and woman as he plants seeds of doubt in their minds (Genesis 3:1). This will remain a primary initial strategy of Satan throughout our history. Much like an initial "air bombardment" to soften the ground for a military campaign, Satan bombards a person's mind with questions designed to

---

[5]The Bible never tells us why this encounter was allowed to happen. Our explanation is simply a human attempt to explain why God may have allowed it, an explanation that makes sense within our overall telling of the story of God's interaction with the world.

weaken faith and bring double-mindedness (a state that James describes as completely unstable – James 1:6–7).

Satan and Independence

The next step in Satan's plan is to lure the man and woman into separating from God and his protection. The success of this step relies on the effectiveness of the first. In the case of Adam and Eve, the first doubts seem to have taken root; when Satan appeals to their pride (or independence), they take the bait and lose the discernment with which they could have resisted his lies. "You won't die!" he hisses. "You will become just like God ..." (Genesis 3:4–5).

"Have your own kingdom," he is telling them. "Become equals with God and have all the benefits that you are currently enjoying without dependence on him." He is not mentioning that the opposite is, in fact, true: If they step away from dependence on God, they will become completely vulnerable – unable to resist Satan's spiritual domination. It is this decision to separate from God and rely instead on our own ability that is the essence of all sin. Sin is not primarily being insufficiently moral or virtuous; it is denying our created dependence on God.

As their pride blinds the discernment of their heart, Adam and Eve take the first bite. With that bite, the cruel reality of Satan's lie is exposed. Separation from God does not bring greater wisdom and power, but a deep, inner experience of alienation. Their independent act causes a ripping of their own hearts that were designed to function in unity with God. Instead of joy and peace, they are filled with confusion and shame. Instead of a sense of security and belonging, there is a deep uncertainty about their identity and purpose. They have rejected God's kingdom, but are powerless to establish their own. As a result, they fall prey to Satan's evil designs.

There is a secondary effect: As the fruit is taken, an immediate and tragic tearing strikes at the heart of the created universe. As God's appointed stewards of the created world, their disobedience affects not just their own lives; the entire creation falls under a curse. Paul describes all creation as "groaning" until this day (Romans 8:19–23). While we can see evidence of God's image, his handprints in humankind and the created order, that image is broken and disfigured.

Satan and Bondage

It is at this point that Satan releases the last step in his strategy: He binds the man and woman with his spiritual power and influence so that they are no longer free to resist his impulses with their will. Directly and indirectly, he begins to increase his influence over them so that God's presence and possible intervention become distanced from them. He works in their minds and will to bring further separation from God and each other and even disintegration within their own personalities (Romans 1:21–32; Ephesians 2:1–3).

When we read the succeeding chapters of Genesis, we see the rapid degeneration that takes place. The idyllic picture of Genesis 2 is shattered. In its place is an escalating breakdown of relationship at all levels. Adam's exclamation of satisfaction at encountering Eve, "bone of my bone," quickly becomes blame shifting, "the woman you gave me". (If you do not trust God and have taken over the judging function, surely he must be to blame for the mistrust that has entered the world!) Soon, one brother is killing another and, within one chapter, descendants are boasting about their violent ways. By the sixth chapter, God's observation of people's hearts reveals that "all their thoughts were consistently and totally evil" (v. 5).

If we continue either to survey the flow of biblical history or to examine the history of humankind from other sources, the same sad story is revealed: The sins of the fathers are visited on their children (Exodus 20:5). Satan exploits the pain and shame of the fall and continues to lie and deceive – offering "solutions" that can medicate but never cure the pain or bring real clarity. These demonic provisions, rather than satisfying, become addictive and ultimately self-destructive. Eventually, long after any pleasure has evaporated, the compulsions remain with all freedom and integrity gone. Such is the power of sin's binding activity that Paul can say we have all become slaves to a sinful nature, unable to free ourselves (Romans 7:18–20). As Adam and Eve immediately discovered, the way back to the garden has been barred; a new way would have to be created.

It is not surprising, then, to see numerous examples in the Old Testament and the New of Satan continuing this basic strategy. In an overall sense, he is simply trying to maintain and even increase the degree of separation from God that he has been able to create in the life of an individual or a community. Sometimes he works directly, utilizing the demonic forces under his control to encourage the growth of the control of sin over people. Perhaps more often, he works indirectly, using the sin in people either to attack and abuse others or to entice them to sinful responses. Over time, he may succeed (and often does) in gaining control over the thinking of a whole community, so that their societal structures become "demonized" in the sense that the worldview of that culture reflects Satan's and not God's values and desires. When that happens, Satan has a powerful external force at his disposal that can either entice or intimidate people into surrendering to his desires. All these influences create the kind of soil in people's lives that is an ideal growth environment for Satan and his demons to plant their seeds of disintegration and eventual death.

We see an example of this process to deceive, separate and bind in the life of the Old Testament Hebrew king, Saul. Though chosen by God, with God's anointing clearly upon him in the early stages of his kingship, Saul struggled with fear and insecurity. His first reply to Samuel upon being chosen as king was: "But I'm only from … the smallest tribe in Israel, and my family is the least important of all the families of that tribe!" (1 Samuel 9:21). When his choice was ratified publicly, his response was to hide among the baggage! The prophet Samuel later identified this inner struggle that Saul had with his own identity and worth (1 Samuel 15:17).

Satan used Saul's insecurities to intimidate him so that he would take matters into his own hands. When Samuel arrived late before a critical battle against the Philistines, Saul acted out what had already become true in his own mind: He trusted in himself more than he trusted in God. Saul's sin separated him from God's authorization and protection and made him even more vulnerable to the oppressive visits of demonic spirits. Rather than truly repenting, Saul took even more rigid control of his life and destiny. At least, that is what he thought he was doing. In reality, Satan was increasing his grip on Saul's life. As Saul's life progresses, we see the mental battle intensifying. Through a tormenting spirit, Satan challenged his faith and filled his mind with doubt and fear. By the end, the man was tragically demonized – estranged from his own family, consumed by rage and fear and, finally, consorting with witchcraft in order to grasp at some measure of control. Deceived, separated and bound.

THE RESTORATION OF JESUS

This process of spiritual decay and bondage is firmly entrenched by the time Jesus makes his pronouncement in Nazareth. Yet in the wisdom of God, this was the perfect time for the Messiah to come (Galatians 4:4). This was the ideal time to plant a different seed – not one of doubt leading to separation and death, but one of hope and faith leading to freedom, reconciliation and eternal life. At first it would be received by just a few, but that reception would be sufficient to produce a wonderful harvest of men and women restored to the joy and freedom of eternal life in God's kingdom.

How did Jesus do this? Through his life and his death, Jesus countered and conquered each of Satan's strategies that had created humanity's bondage:

- Satan came with doubt and deception; Jesus invariably spoke the truth.
- Satan's goal was always separation from God through these lies; like a shepherd, Jesus' goal was to find the lost sheep and bring them home.

- Satan's ultimate intention was disintegration and destruction; Jesus came to bring freedom.

Let's look at each of these in turn.

Jesus and Truth

> And you will know the truth, and the truth will set you free. (John 8:32)

First, in contrast to the deceiver, Jesus walked in absolute integrity in his relationships with others. He always spoke truth and never deceived or manipulated. He said: "I am the way, the truth and the life" (John 14:6), drawing a contrast between himself and Satan, the "father of lies" (John 8:44). He never told people what they wanted to hear, he told them what they needed to hear – how to turn and be freed from their bondage and oppression. Yet his truthfulness was always clothed in unconditional love and acceptance; it was an invitation to life and hope, not simply harsh condemnation.

The story of the Samaritan woman at the well in Sychar in John 4 illustrates this magnificently. At first glance, the reason for Jesus' return to Galilee that sets up this encounter seems to be simple necessity: Samaria lies between Judea and Galilee to the north, hence "he had to go through Samaria" (v. 4). This assumes that a straight line and shortest distance was the highest priority. For many religious leaders, particularly the Pharisees, their animosity toward the half-breed Samaritans (a feeling that was reciprocated) and their fear of becoming "unclean" through contact with them, motivated them to choose a much longer, circuitous route.

Why did Jesus have to go through Samaria? My suspicion is that his Father had spoken to him about an important encounter there – an encounter that God would make sure was recorded (in this case by John) so that people would be better able to understand his heart for real intimacy based on truthful exchange.

As the story unfolds, we find Jesus, who is tired and hungry, sitting alone at the village well. This is not surprising. It is noon – the heat of the day. Watering duties were fulfilled in the cooler hours of the morning and evening. (The disciples were given an interesting challenge: Find a kosher meal in a Samaritan village. A bit, I suppose, like trying to order organic at a fast-food restaurant.)

Soon the reason for this "necessary" journey stumbles onto Jesus: A Samaritan woman comes to draw water at a highly unusual time. It is so unusual, in fact, that we must wonder why she would not only forego what was a prime socializing time for village women, but actively avoid it. She would have recognized immediately by Jesus' dress that he was Jewish and she would have been aware of a typical, daily rabbinic recitation: "Thank you, God, that I was not made a Gentile, a woman or a dog." She was probably quite relieved that this man would not initiate a conversation with her. No doubt she went about her duties quietly.

When Jesus asked her for a drink, she was suitably shocked – he was acting completely out of character. She was so taken aback that she could not help but ask him about it: "Why are you breaking the rules? Certainly you know who I am," she may have thought. At the same time she may have been quite thankful that, as an outsider, he would not be fully aware of her reputation. Jesus turned the tables on her: "If you knew me and the invitation that my

Father wants to release through me, you would be begging me for a drink – in this case, for living water."

We must consider the woman's likely response to this dialogue, especially the part about living water. No doubt she would have responded immediately, "Oh, I understand! You must be referring to the prophecy by Isaiah (Isaiah 58:11) of an inner source of life springing up within like a well full of water. You must be the promised one sent to release God's Spirit to live within each person (that is, of course, "once you have been glorified", if I understand the New Covenant correctly)." No! More likely, she simply nodded quietly (she was, after all, the one in the inferior social position), not having a clue what he was talking about. (Living water ... running water from a well?) Nevertheless, she continued to dialogue: "How are you going to come up with this water and how is it going to improve magically what we have always drawn from this well?" Jesus' response about water that becomes its own internal well once it enters a person makes no rational sense. Hindsight makes it easy for us to make the spiritual application, but there is no reason to believe that the woman could do so easily – as far as she knew, they were still speaking of literal water!

What, then, kept her in the conversation? Why did she not simply dismiss this strange man, who was either deluded or else cruelly stringing her along? There must have been a dynamic at work that went beyond words; she was in the company of the One through whom all life has come to be. The hunger of her heart had been called out and she responded in trust: "Please, sir, give me some of that water!"

It is at this point that there is a dramatic shift in the conversation. On one level, it would only be appropriate, as it would be considered improper for Jesus to carry on much of a conversation with a woman without the presence of her husband. In this case, however, there is another reason: The invitation Jesus extended is really that first expressed in Isaiah 55 finding its full expression in him. The water offered is the covenant of God's love for us; it is an invitation to come back to the intimate relationship with God that was lost in the garden. And while it is absolutely free (meaning that anyone can receive it), it does have a cost: We must receive it just as we are – without pretensions, in full, honest recognition of our inability to earn it.

For the woman, it was important to realize that Jesus knew exactly who she was and what she had done and that he made his offer on the basis of that understanding. Perhaps, when he first asked, "Go and get your husband," she caught herself, realizing that she had uncharacteristically let down her guard, risking vulnerability. There was a reason why she had come to draw water in the middle of the day; that reason stemmed from the answer to Jesus' question.

"I don't have a husband," the woman replied. In fact, Jesus pointed out, she had had five husbands and was living in a relationship with a sixth without the "honour" of a marriage. As we have discussed, this was a woman who, for whatever reasons, had been shunned by all respectable people in the village. Everyone knew the "truth" about this woman and no doubt it had been the topic of many conversations – a "truth" that this woman probably believed about herself, which set her up for one rejection after another. At the very least she, as well as the others, would see herself as being under the judgment of God. I imagine that Jesus' response shocked her back into reality: What a wonderful invitation this was (the longing of her heart), but she did not qualify – her past failure and sinfulness disqualified her.

Yet her reply to Jesus is surprising. Rather than simply withdrawing in shame, retreating to the same isolation that she had used to cope over the years, she continued to engage with Jesus. Some think she tried to regain some control in the situation by switching the topic and discussing theology (a great way to avoid dealing with how we really are!). I believe differently. Perhaps she saw that his look did not condemn her; he was not like the others. Certainly he was a prophet, but if that was so, he made this invitation knowing the truth about her. Could that be true? If so, how could it be realized?

I think her response about the real way to worship can be paraphrased like this: "I'm not a theologian (it all confuses me), but you obviously know how to please God and become a true worshipper of him … will you tell me how?" This is exactly what Jesus did. The Jews had been nearer to God's ways and the Samaritans further away, he said, and yet all of that was making way for a new age of invitation based on spirit and truth. The desire of God's heart is real relationship with individuals who will come to him honestly, just as they are, welcoming him into the most intimate part of their lives. This worship is to be a connection of spirit to spirit, not just the external fulfilment of a ritual.

Jesus was not just talking theoretically about this new covenant; he was extending an invitation to this woman to experience it, and that was not lost on her. Jesus truly became "the way, the truth and the life" (John 14:6) for her by telling her who she could be if she came to God just as she was. This was truth as a powerful spiritual weapon

(Hebrews 4:12) that cut through the cords of deception and rejection and, in this case, set the woman absolutely free – so free that she spontaneously proclaimed to the whole village: "Come and meet a man who told me everything I ever did! Can this be the Messiah?" (John 4:29). The transformation in this woman was so obvious and compelling that many in the village were touched by this invitation of truth that came through Jesus and believed in him. (Could the woman's live-in have been one of them? If so, what a wonderful wedding there would have been in Sychar!)

Jesus and Reconciliation

Second, whereas Satan's central intention has always been to build walls of separation (first between people and God, then between people and finally, even within their own personality and sense of identity), Jesus came to tear these walls down. "He has broken down the wall of hostility that used to separate us," is the way Paul describes it in Ephesians 2:14. While Satan's ultimate goal is hell or "outer darkness" (billions of people absolutely isolated and alone),[6] Jesus' goal is the fully revealed kingdom of God (multitudes completely united in an eternal community of love).

Satan's primary strategy has always been to divide and conquer: By isolating people, he can minimize the synergistic strength that comes from unity (Ecclesiastes 4:12)

---

[6]There are two pictures of hell in the New Testament. One is "outer darkness" or total separation (Matthew 8:12); the other is destruction, often pictured using the garbage fires that burned in the Valley of Gehenna (Matthew 25:41). Both are metaphors and neither is pleasant. In this case, we are focusing on the former metaphor rather than the latter.

and more easily gain advantage over them. In contrast, Jesus never grasped for power or position. As Paul explains in Colossians 1:15, he is already "supreme over all creation" and "everything has been created through him and for him". Philippians 2 tells us that his purpose in coming to earth was not to use his divine attributes to re-establish control; he relinquished his divine rights and prerogatives and willingly took the most humble position imaginable. Though fully God, he took on himself all the limitations of being human, living among us so that he could show his love for us in the way he served and laid down his life.

He did not do this to be particularly noble, but because becoming representatively human was the only possible way that we could be reconciled with him. Without his initiative, our situation was hopeless. On our own, we could not and would not find our way back to the garden, the place of restored relationship with our Maker. God either had to reach out to us or he would have to abandon us – there was no other way.

This is the great mystery of the Scriptures. As we read the Old Testament account of the fall, along with the disintegration of humanity that followed, we can't help but come to the conclusion that the human condition is beyond salvaging, much like a car that has been in such a collision that it is beyond repair. "Write it off!" we would say. No one could fault God if that was the decision he came to. It would be perfectly just and sensible.

The way I see it, God created everything in six days the first time; he could probably do it in three the second time around! Weigh that against the incredible task of redemption, spanning thousands of years and unbelievable pain and cost (for people and for God) – not to mention the total humiliation that God would have to endure in paying the price for our rebellion. C.S. Lewis's description of the death of Aslan in the Narnia Chronicles gives us a glimpse of some of the spiritual cost. At the same time, we must not underestimate the emotional cost of being hostilely rejected by the very ones you have paid the greatest price to rescue. When we truly consider the extent of Jesus' sacrifice in reclaiming us, we begin to understand the depth of God's love for us (1 John 3:16; 2 Corinthians 8:9).

In 2 Corinthians 8, Paul's description of Jesus becoming poor goes beyond surrendering the riches of heaven. He lived and worked among the oppressed poor and tangibly embraced the marginalized. We cannot read the Bible without recognizing God's passionate anger against injustice or his heart for the marginalized and oppressed (Job 34:28; Amos 5:21–24; Isaiah 41:17; Luke 4:18; James 2:5). In Jesus, we see this heart perfectly expressed: His actions proclaim that every created person is of immense value to God, especially those seen and treated as worthless by society. He announces a kingdom that is truly upside-down when compared to our earthly hierarchies – a kingdom where the first are last and the last first (Matthew 20:16). When justice is fully restored and the King's rule is established, there will be no need for jockeying for power and control or for manipulating and dominating others. In the security of God's authority, each one can be embraced and valued for who they are rather than as a means to an end.

This is diametrically opposed to Satan's goal of encouraging ruthless competition. His efforts and strategies lie under the surface of all oppressive regimes, whether overt or subtle. In societies based on rankings, most are condemned to be losers in the system, many harshly so. At their core, these structures pit one against another, destroying true community and leaving individuals to cope on their own. "Am I my brother's keeper?" is all too typical a response that epitomizes the general passivity with regard to one another that marks our competitive culture.

Jesus is anything but passive in his relentless pursuit of reconciled relationship with us. He seems little concerned for his rights and is totally secure in his position and power. His heart is that of a faithful shepherd: When a sheep is lost, his primary concern is to find that sheep and restore it. He reveals the true Father, who does not compete with his children, but is committed to intimate relationship with them. He loves them unconditionally.

This heart of God for reconciliation (perfectly expressed through Jesus) is wonderfully illustrated in a series of Jesus' stories recorded by Luke in his Gospel (chapter 15). The setting is a familiar one: The religious "performers" (the Pharisees and teachers of religious law) are criticizing Jesus for hanging out with the wrong people. These people are the ones who have failed to measure up ("notorious sinners … despicable people" is the Pharisees' description) and should therefore be rejected and avoided. In response, Jesus tells three stories to show them that God's values are different to theirs. (I'm sure he was also telling these stories for the benefit of the other listening audience – the tax collectors, prostitutes and others who responded wholeheartedly to his invitation.)

The third story, a story of a father and his two sons, is the longest and would have had the most powerful impact. Very quickly, Jesus introduces a major, scandalous conflict.

The younger son tells his father: "I want my share of your estate now, instead of waiting until you die" (Luke 15:12). Everyone in the audience would have understood immediately that the son was completely out of line. No father would be expected to go along with such an audacious power play. In the traditional patriarchal system, a son remained under the authority of the father's house until the death of his father. Even when he married, he and his wife would simply move into new rooms built onto the father's house (assuming that the family was wealthy enough to afford the luxury of another room). Such an ultimatum was almost unthinkable and everyone would have expected the father to dismiss it out of hand.

Jesus followed immediately with the shocking statement: "So his father agreed." What could possibly motivate a father to act this way? "Most likely weakness," the listeners would imagine. "It will most certainly end badly!" And end badly it did. It is a true worst-case scenario: The son squandered his entire inheritance. And, in what would be the ultimate humiliation for a Hebrew family, in desperation he took employment at a hog farm. When pig food looks good to a Jewish boy, he has hit bottom!

At this point, the unworthy son recognized how completely he had blown it. He understood (and Jesus' listeners would concur) that all hope of things being restored to their original state was lost; he could not regain his status as a son. Instead, knowing the vastly better state of his father's servants, he hatched a desperate plot. Perhaps his father would hire him. He knew that the odds against it were significant. He had greatly humiliated his father and no doubt had been disowned. Perhaps if he could show suitable repentance, there might be a chance. And it was that chance that motivated him to begin the long journey home.

As he neared his father's property, I can imagine him rehearsing his lines, "Father, I have sinned." He would likely have only a brief chance and would have to make the most of it. He looked up for a moment during his rehearsal, and what he saw must have struck terror into his heart. His father was running toward him!

To many of us, a father running would not seem so strange, but in Hebrew society in the ancient Near East, it would be virtually unthinkable for a father to do so in this situation. Many others would run in service of the father: Servants would run, women would run, children would too, but the father would walk. It would be beneath his dignity to show this much haste. What could possibly have motivated this father to run? In the mind of the failed son, perhaps only one thing: He was so angry with his son for the shame he had brought on the family, that he was running to exact vengeance.

As the father came close, perhaps the son dropped to his knees and began his practiced confession: "Father, I have sinned against both heaven and you, and I am not worthy of being called your son." But he was unable to discuss his proposal for a contractual relationship. The father had something completely different in mind from what either the son or Jesus' listeners could have imagined. While the son was a long distance away, the father saw him. Most likely that was the case because the father was searching the horizon for him and had been doing so since he had left. When he saw his son, his immediate response was not anger or a desire for retribution, but love and compassion.

It is this overwhelming love and care for his lost son that caused the father to forget his dignity and convention and race toward his son to welcome and embrace him.

The father was not thinking about making room in the servants' quarters. He immediately called for a robe, a ring and sandals. His heart for his son was not a contractual relationship based on performance, but an unconditional covenant. It could bend (there can be consequence for diso-bedience), but it could never break. Restoration depended only on the repentant return of the son; there was never any question or hesitation in the father's heart. "We must celebrate with a feast, for this son of mine was dead and has now returned to life. He was lost, but now he is found."

The reaction of Jesus' critics to this story was much like that of the second son, who is now introduced: Never under-standing the generous, loving heart of his father for him, he responded competitively. The calf that was being slaughtered was from his half of the inheritance! He hadn't understood the father's heart for covenant and couldn't embrace it for his brother. Ironically, at the end of the story, the lost brother was the one who supposedly never left at all.

Jesus came to reveal this passionate concern of God for reconciliation with his lost children. He disregarded the traditional walls of separation and "ran" toward lost, broken sinners with that heart.

Jesus and Freedom

Finally, Jesus directly confronted the spiritual, physical and emotional strongholds of Satan's rule in the lives of people. In Acts 10:38, Luke quotes Peter describing this aspect of the ministry of Jesus to Cornelius: "And no doubt you know that God anointed Jesus of Nazareth with the Holy Spirit and with power. Then Jesus went around doing good and healing all who were oppressed by the devil, for God was with him."

Jesus recognized that much of the brokenness and "dis-ease" of people is a natural consequence of a fallen world, separated from the life of God. Jesus came to reverse those consequences – through him the kingdom and rule of God had come near with multifaceted salvation. It is not surprising that much of his ministry was directed at overturning those situations by healing the sick, restoring relationships and supplying miraculous provision. Jesus knew that often Satan and his forces were directly oppressing and binding the lives of these people.

When Jesus recognized that a physical symptom was primarily a spiritual affliction, he rebuked that stronghold and, whether explicitly mentioned or by inference, the spirit behind it, setting the afflicted one free. In Luke 13, we read of Jesus encountering a woman in the synagogue who had been bent double for eighteen years. Though there could have been a purely physiological explanation for her condition, Jesus knew by discernment that the primary cause of this problem was an evil spirit. He called her over, touched her and spoke words of release over her, setting her free from this bondage of Satan (as he described it after the fact).

There appears to be a variety of approaches in the way Jesus would release people from these strongholds:

- Sometimes he simply seemed to address the outward condition.
- At other times, he rebuked the spirit directly (Luke 9:42).

- In certain cases, he rebuked the spirit repeatedly over a period of time (Luke 8:29, 31).

Perhaps this is due to the various levels and degrees of demonic control. In certain situations, the main presenting symptom of affliction by a spirit is physical. In others, it can range from periodic loss of control to severely, powerfully directed behaviour where the spirit regularly seems to be able to express its personality through the person. Whether or not these evil spirits are in, on or around people is not made clear; nor is the precise language that is needed for bringing freedom. What is essential is that Jesus knew that he had authority over these spirits and their effects (Luke 4:18; 11:14–22; Mark 1:21–28) and that, irrespective of the exact language he used, the evil spirits would have to release what they had plundered. He had the full backing of heaven.

We see this in the story of the man Jesus encountered in the region of the Gerasenes (Mark 5:1–20). This man probably represents the most extreme example of full demonization. There seem to be very few times when the spirits that afflicted the man did not have full control over his personality. The result of this stronghold had been devastating; it had cost him virtually everything. It had separated him from all relationship and kept him in constant torment and self-abuse. We discover the reason for such profound personal destruction: Whether we take one thousand to be literal or figurative, a large number of demons were afflicting him. No wonder he could not be restrained or controlled by anyone – he was demonically empowered.

As Jesus and the disciples stepped from the boat, the first thing they saw was this man. Like the father in the previous story, this man was running to meet them. I can't imagine the disciples being very excited about the sight of this man (he must have looked terrifying) or about his intentions. If they had had any prior information concerning his history, they would have been back in the boat, paddling furiously.

As we hear the story, our first reaction is also to anticipate major conflict – no doubt this demonized man is going to try to attack Jesus. But if we reflect for a moment, we realize how unlikely this would be. Throughout the Gospel accounts, whenever there is an encounter between Jesus and demons, all movement involving demons is away from Jesus. As James reminds us in his letter, demons tremble in terror at the power of God (James 2:19). It is not surprising that whenever they are in the presence of Jesus, God's chosen agent to express his rule, they try desperately to escape.

How does this relate to the present story? As Jesus stepped ashore, the demons (perhaps up to one thousand of them) were no doubt keen to go in the opposite direction to avoid a confrontation with the One whose purpose was to destroy them (Mark 1:24; 1 John 3:8). How astonishing it is then that this man, who was completely powerless to exert his own will in the face of the demonic stronghold that ruled over him, was able to drag a thousand demons, kicking and screaming, to the feet of Jesus. There was something so powerful in the presence of Jesus as he approached this man, that as it touched something deep within his spirit, nothing could prevent him from responding to that invitation.

Jesus' mere presence set the man free enough to come and bow before him in an appeal for deliverance. With his heart so engaged, it was just a matter of time before he was cleansed and restored. So it is with every man and woman who receives God's invitation: If their hearts respond, there are not enough demons in hell to keep them from coming to his feet and being set free.

FOLLOWING THE EXAMPLE OF JESUS

As Jesus' disciples, charged with continuing his ministry today, we are well advised to focus on the strategies he modelled for us. We are to use the weapons that he used to break down the devil's strongholds (2 Corinthians 10:4), countering his strategies just as Jesus did. We are to walk in truth and use God's truth as a powerful spiritual laser, penetrating dungeons of deception. We are to embrace the reconciling spirit of Jesus and resist the passivity of our individualistic culture by actively reaching across dividing barriers to the marginalized. Confident in the authority that Jesus has given us to heal the sick, free the prisoners and release the oppressed, we can speak with certainty to spiritual strongholds just as Moses did to Pharaoh: "This is what the LORD, the God of Israel, says: 'Let my people go …'" (Exodus 5:1).

The Power of Truth

If we are to bring the Good News of the kingdom to the oppressed effectively, we must understand the power of the truth, base our lives and thinking on it and be able to speak it with authority. This means cultivating an ever-deepening relationship with Jesus, who is truth embodied. It also means faithfully studying and meditating on the Scriptures, the soil of truth out of which the Holy Spirit speaks and guides (2 Timothy 3:16). With this foundation established in us, we can anticipate gifts of both wisdom and revelation from the Spirit to assist us in penetrating spiritual strongholds of deception that keep people in bondage.

Knowing God's truth is the key to freedom (John 8:32). At the core of this truth is the reality that humankind was created to live in harmony with and dependence on God. What we call independence (a goal highly valued in our culture) is actually a place of great vulnerability and deception, as Adam and Eve discovered in the garden. This is indeed the central issue of all sin: The idea that human beings could rule without submission to the rule of God. Independence rather than wrongdoing is the essence of sin.

As long as any remnant of God's image remains in his created ones, the understanding that we are created for dependence on God remains deep within the human heart, even if it is suppressed and largely dormant. Since the Creator of this image lives in us, we can expect strong authority to call this "memory" to life in others. This is especially so when our words and the modelling of our life choices join in a singular voice and we become living examples of what restored relationship with God, and the freedom that it brings, looks like.

Usually when people speak of "telling the truth", it is a negative experience, reminding others of what isn't and who they are not. It is usually associated with failure and rejection. Our ministry of truth is very different: It is centred on who we can be when we walk into the freedom of dependence on and restored relationship with God. As Paul describes in Colossians 1, it is not just a journey out of the kingdom of darkness, but also a journey into the kingdom of God's Son. The truth of God is a profound invitation into who we are in his image and who we can become.

Some years ago, a young man attended one of my workshops on spiritual warfare in Singapore. He came from a very broken and abusive past and had become a Christian a few years before. Since that time, he had really struggled with demonic oppression – so much so that he had never gone through a corporate worship time without experiencing such dramatic manifestations of these spirits that he had to be removed from the public meeting. What invariably followed was a "deliverance session", where he was pinned down on the floor by a number of well-meaning "ministers," who spent an hour shouting at him and commanding the demons to leave. When the spirits had the good sense to take cover, the session would be pronounced a success. However, when the coast was clear, the demons would simply reassert their control, waiting for the next round of confrontation. After years of this, the poor man seldom attended any kind of public gathering out of hopelessness, fear and shame. He had long since lost hope that the Good News of Jesus could be of much benefit to him.

When we began a time of worship in our workshop, the predictable happened and he needed to be taken out of the session. When I later joined the people that had gone out to pray with him, we decided to "divide up the teams" in a slightly different fashion to what he had become accustomed. We put him on our team, along with the Holy Spirit, working together with him instead of praying "at" him and treating him as a demonized victim, powerless to participate with us until he had been set free. We commanded the spirits to stay to the sidelines while we began to affirm from Scripture who he was in Christ and who he was becoming. We then led him in a process of discerning, with the help of the Holy Spirit, just what was harassing him and through what circumstances it had gained a foothold.

By leading him through acts of repentance, submitting himself to the rule of God in those areas, we effectively cut off the "handles" that these demonic powers used to rattle him. Then, with our encouragement and prayer support, he took his authority as a child of God, chosen by the Father, and he commanded each spirit to leave him and cease to harass him. To his amazement, over a period of the next hour or so, he was set free – without a single shout! Even better, however, he was built up in his identity as one of God's own and he was quite convinced that if these demons harassed him again, he would be able to resist them. It was a very joyful time for all of us to see him later, worshipping in the community of God's people with tears of gratitude streaming down his face. The truth that set him free was seeing who he could become in partnership with God's Spirit.

When we speak these things, we do so with great authority and power. God's truth is not just good information. "The word of God is full of living power. It is sharper than the sharpest knife, cutting deep into our innermost thoughts and desires. It exposes us for what we really are" (Hebrews 4:12). We can rely on the Holy Spirit to bring to our minds those parts of Scripture that will cut through webs of deception and bring the light of truth, making repentance possible.

Sometimes, in addition to this kind of Holy Spirit-inspired wisdom, we receive spiritual revelation. God's Spirit can give us specific insight and information that we could not know by any natural means, that powerfully opens up a person's heart to God's truth (as we discussed in Chapter 3).

A good friend, Dan Wilt, had an experience like this as he was enjoying one of his frequent activities, flying. Here's how Dan describes what happened to him:

I was on an airplane, preparing for a quiet and reflective trip, when a loud, boisterous man came bustling on board. The only seat available in the plane was right beside me, and everything in me was hoping that my blissful reading plans would not be interrupted by hours of conversation. He sat down beside me, and within a few minutes was asking me about my faith – doggedly and with a touch of belligerence. An angry agnostic, he felt that his little girl, who lay dying in a hospital, had been duped into believing that her mission on earth was to heal others. She regularly moved around the sick children's ward of the hospital, praying for those little ones living in so much pain and uncertainty. Her capacity to comfort others disturbed him, and created for him the image of a twisted and schizophrenic God who neither hears nor acts on the cries of people.

After a few hours of monologue (his, not mine), he began to confess to me that, ten years earlier, he had been ordered to murder individually eight drug lord underlings in a Central American country at the bidding of his commander. He said that he had never told anyone else this dark fact, but he somehow felt safe, and referred to me being "like a priest". (I still had not told him that I did any ministry work vocationally – he was too focused to ask me about my life.) His life, stained with blood decades later, must now be spent in restitution, he declared – saving at least eight lives before he dies. Serving on a rescue team in the mountains, he was committed to assuaging his guilt by doing his own internal penance – and leaving room for the fact that his guilt may or may not be held against him in the afterlife.

For two hours, he described bitterly his hatred of God (It's my understanding that someone has to exist for another to be angry at them!), his mistrust of authority, his anger over his little girl's disease and his life in the fast lane. Then, the voice of God whispered to me: "Look for the image." I almost had to shake my head to reorient my mind's eye. I slowly began to see this angry man with love, and a deep compassion brimmed in my heart for him and his little girl.

Then God spoke again: "Ask him about Rachel." Rachel was not a name that had come up in our conversation, and I knew that God was either precipitating a power encounter in the back of that airplane, or I was actually listening to one of the three hundred and forty-seven voices I hear buzzing in my brain daily!

Standing on the edge of a spiritual cliff, I asked him, "Who is Rachel and what place does she have in your life?"

His jaw slackened, his eyes grew wide and his voice began to tremble. "How do you know Rachel?" he asked, his lip quivering. I explained that I believe that God speaks to people, and that he had a message he wanted to speak to a broken son who sees no way out of the present trap he is in. As tears began to flow freely now, he explained that Rachel was his present girlfriend, a spiritually-seeking Catholic woman who was pestering him with Jesus-talk at every turn. He was about to break up with her upon his arrival at our destination.

For the next few hours, we talked about who God is, who Christ is and how God was subverting his worldview through his daughter and girlfriend. Broken by the fact that God would tell me the name of his girlfriend to get his attention, he hugged me and declared that the next few days would be spent re-evaluating his beliefs about God being near, and welcoming a spiritual change in his life.

What do these two stories tell us about the power of God's truth? Simply this: Just as Satan sows seeds of doubt to begin his process of destruction, the truth that comes from God begins to crack the seemingly secure walls of spiritual dungeons so that the captives can be released.

Ambassadors of Reconciliation

Probably no man in Scripture understood the power of truth to overpower deception better than the great early leader of the church, Paul (formerly Saul, the Pharisee). His zealous persecution of the Christian sect was, for him, a passionate defence of God's honour against this false prophet Jesus and his followers, who were claiming that he had risen from the dead and was exalted to God's right hand. It never entered his mind that this claim could be true or that he could be deceived.

I can imagine Saul's thoughts as he approached Damascus at the heart of his campaign. I'm sure at times he wished that he had been younger and could have met this man Jesus personally – he would have stopped this heresy before it had gained momentum. Whether that was really running through his mind or not, according to Acts 9, that is exactly what took place: He encountered a brilliant light from heaven that blinded him and knocked him to the ground.

At this point, Saul heard a voice coming from heaven. As a Pharisee, he would have been familiar with the potential danger of such an encounter. Of three rabbinical accounts of these kinds of experiences, one rabbi had escaped relatively unscathed, one had lost his mind and the last had simply perished! Certainly, he would have hoped that his ardent crusade on behalf of God would place him in a favourable light. However, when the voice began to speak, Saul knew that he was finished. The voice from heaven was that of Jesus. Saul had made the gravest mistake possible – he had become an active enemy of God himself.

Saul understood that he was a dead man. He was very familiar with the God of the Old Testament and realized that this intervention of God must be for the purpose of executing judgment. The only thing he was not sure of was exactly how he was going to die. He realized that God had a variety of options from which to choose: He could send fire from heaven, the ground could open up and swallow him or a lion could come and tear him to pieces. While I'm sure Saul would have had his preferences, he wasn't in a strong bargaining position.

Saul was partially right in his assessment of what God intended to do. In a sense, he was "killed"; from this time he would always speak about this experience as the end of one life and the beginning of a next. Yet it was with mercy and kindness that God brought about this change, not judgment. As the truth penetrated the deception that had driven him, his entire focus shifted. God had truly captured his heart. His central motivation was now to respond to this love that had come to him so unexpectedly. He said:

"Whatever we do, it is because Christ's love controls us" (2 Corinthians 5:14). From this point on, what Saul, later Paul, cared about increasingly were the concerns of God's heart. His consuming passion was to bring others to this same great mercy that had reconciled him.

And, Paul would say, this is precisely what God wants to bring about in all of us who have been similarly redeemed from deception and separation. God has commissioned and authorized us to act as his ambassadors of reconciliation, extending the offer of God's free gift of grace through Jesus (2 Corinthians 5:18–21). When the desires of God's heart and gratitude for his kindness take root in us, this is a privilege, not some obligatory "project" for God.

The invitation that we extend in God's name is free, but not cheap. The Good News of Jesus is that God is near (Mark 1:15), not far away, and that through him, God is making an amazing offer of restoration. The cost? Simply believe in its veracity, turn completely from trying to live independently of God and pledge yourself to Jesus as your leader. In this sense, the offer of reconciliation is the great leveller: Anyone can afford it, simply because it costs you everything you have. We can, with all the authority of heaven, pronounce to people that God's intention is no longer to count their sins against them (total amnesty). But the door to responding to such an invitation is complete and total surrender.

We know that Satan's primary preoccupation is keeping that offer from being clearly seen and believed. What can we do to increase the likelihood that the message will be heard and received? We can embrace the attitude and example of Jesus described in Philippians 2. Though "he was God, he did not demand and cling to his rights as God" (Philippians 2:6). He stepped into the space that existed between us ("emptied himself" is how the theologians describe it). He didn't wait for the impossible, i.e. for us to find a way to him, but intentionally and actively came to us in our lost and broken state. In paying the greatest possible relational cost, he proved his love for us. This is why the marginalized outcasts of society in his day recognized him as their friend.

It is this heart of Jesus that motivates Paul to make the greatest sacrifices possible – persecution and imprisonment, physical hardships such as shipwrecks, beatings and starvation, and rejection. What is his reward? The legacy of thousands being freed and restored to the grace of God (2 Corinthians 4). To this end, he worked tirelessly and counted his sacrifice and suffering as the greatest privilege.

I have two modern-day heroes that, in my view, have exemplified this as well as anyone I have ever met. Joyce Heron and Katherine Bentham are two young women who are making a significant difference in two of the most broken communities in Canada. They have dedicated their lives to living out Jesus' example with the "notorious sinners" of our day: The heroin addicts and sex trade workers of the inner city. Both these women and their teams of volunteers have, in their respective communities, put hands and feet to Jesus' offer of real friendship. Their work is not a project; it is relationship that, while at times overwhelming, is always a privilege.

All the quick answers have been tried and have failed in the Downtown Eastside of Vancouver where Joyce lives and works. Deep repentance that leads to true reconciliation cannot result from a project. What is needed is an incarnational invitation of God's heart. Joyce describes what she and her team of coworkers are trying to do:

> Scripture seems to demonstrate that God has a bias toward the poor, the downtrodden, the oppressed, and the folk on the periphery of society that we often ignore. It might not be a grace bias, but it's one that means he has a heightened sense of protectiveness toward them. It's similar to a father who finds out that one of his children is being mercilessly picked on at school. Although he loves all his children equally, he may go out of his way for that one particular daughter or son to bring care and love to them. This is the bias that motivates my life, and the life of our community at Jacob's Well. We want to engage our lives in ways that break off the heavy yoke and set the oppressed free. We want to be announcers and demonstrators of Good News.
>
> The difficulty is that most people think that the way to go about bringing this Good News is by setting up a bunch of programs. I'm convinced most of the time that only serves to create further alienation … a pronounced "us and them". Jesus demonstrated genuine friendship with the "sinners" of his day and I think he calls us to the same. So, our goal is just to love and to build meaningful friendships with folk in our neighbourhood. Not a downward relating type of stance. Everyone needs loving human relationship, more than anything else.
>
> In our neighbourhood you can get fed seven times a day, but you'll have a really difficult time finding a friend you can trust day in and day out. It's these friendships we've been building the past few years that are changing us, and changing our friends. It never ceases to amaze

me how I can meet Christ in one of my crack-addicted friends or find the Holy Spirit teaching me through a friend who suffers deeply with mental illness. And I could tell you countless stories of our friends who are discovering Jesus through this love they feel in our community. This is the mystery of the kingdom. God's treasure is hidden in people, especially those on the margins of society whom he so deeply loves.[7]

Far too often the image that comes to mind when we speak about this call to repentance is exactly the opposite of what we have just described: We see uncaring, disengaged "prophetic" figures giving the bad news of a frustrated and angry God – a distortion that they well represent! As Bill Hybels stresses: "The lost matter to God!"[8] Only once we have fully caught that passion in God's heart will we be ready, like shepherds, to bring the lost ones home.

Freedom to the Captives

"Humble yourselves before God," says James. (4:7–8). "Resist the devil, and he will flee from you. Draw close to God, and God will draw close to you." When anyone hears the Good News of the kingdom and turns to it in repentance, the rule of God comes to their aid. That is, and always has been, bad news for God's enemy. Jesus made it clear to those who misunderstood his encounters with demonic strongholds: These were clear signs that God's kingdom was present in

---

[7]You can find out more about Jacob's Well (Joyce and team) at www.jacobswell.ca and Hope in Action (Katherine and team) at www.hopeinaction.com.
[8]Bill Hybels and Mark Mittleberg, *Becoming a Contagious Christian* (Grand Rapids: Zondervan, 1996).

him (Luke 11:20–22). Since we are called to this same ministry, we can expect the same kind of authorization.

Jesus has commissioned us to continue his mission – we confront the "strong man" guarding his ill-gotten plunder, the lives of God's created ones, in his name. It is not surprising, then, that when Paul turns to the demonically controlled slave girl and says: "I command you in the name of Jesus Christ to come out of her," she is instantly set free (Acts 16:18). We can expect this to be our experience too when we confront Satan's bondage and affliction in others. When people draw near to Jesus, we can speak with his authority and simply rebuke the various forms of oppression that harass them – whether the effect is primarily spiritual, physical or emotional.

Just such a powerful experience of freedom came to this woman from the American Midwest as she was prayed for at a conference hosted by one of my Vineyard colleagues. Here is her story, in her own words:

> I originally went to the seminar on spiritual warfare just to learn more about it. To be honest, I was struggling with accepting the idea of demonic oppression and for some reason, it just really frightened me. Days before the seminar date, I began to question whether or not I should go. I just had these feelings and thoughts that I shouldn't and had unexplainable crying spells. I talked myself into it, saying I would at least go to the first night of the seminar to check it out.
>
> I was fine during the worship and lecture part, but when the ministry time began, things changed fast. When I heard and saw a person shrieking in a way I just knew wasn't human, I felt like I had never been more

terrified in my life. I felt as though a gallon of adrenalin had been dumped into me and I was trembling uncontrollably. I have felt the presence of the Spirit before, and this definitely wasn't it. All I wanted to do was run away. I kept getting thoughts that I would be laughed at if I asked for prayer, that I would look foolish if I actually screamed and that I was simply imagining all of this – these thoughts were definitely not my own! I recalled 2 Timothy 1:7 and I knew that I needed to make it up front. By the time I got there, I could barely speak because I was concentrating so hard on trying not to shake too badly.

Thankfully, I didn't need to speak that much to the person who came to pray for me because he had already received some revelation from God concerning my condition. He asked me if my parents were involved in any unusual religions. I was surprised he asked: My family background was Jewish, but my father was and still is heavily involved in Hindu beliefs. I had personally been to India twice in my life to stay at an ashram because of my father's involvement.

As the person began to pray for me, I remember him saying, "In Jesus' name, I command the spirit of 'kundalini' to come out!" My physical response to the word, "kundalini", was shocking. I instantly jerked forward and I could feel my face twisting into a grimace. I don't know if he had encountered people who have had "kundalini" awakening problems before or if that name came by revelation. I never really knew much about it other than it was a "serpentine" energy that is said to dwell in the lower back of people, waiting to be awakened so that it may open "chakras".

I really didn't understand my reaction to that word until I went home. I suddenly remembered how my father had told me once that a guru had laid hands on my mother's stomach while I was still in the womb, and "blessed" me with this energy. I believe that this spirit has affected me for all of my life. I can now understand some of the things I have struggled with in the past, mainly anxiety.

I don't really know how long the process of releasing me from that spirit's control took after that, though I do know that I became aware of two others at some point praying as well. What I do know for a fact is this – when I woke up the next morning, I knew everything had changed! Everything in me and around me was clean, safe and joyful. I felt as if that day was the first day of a whole new life. I felt as though I had been taken off life-support. I finally understood what Charles Finney meant in describing an infilling of the Spirit as "waves of liquid love". I could feel that ecstatic presence. It just all clicked. God was finally fully in my heart as well as my head. I went to the second half of the seminar and waited to see how I would respond to the ministry time. I was so happy to see people being freed that I was clapping with others!

A Canadian pastor shares a similar story of instantaneous, dramatic change when someone laid their hands on him and spoke similar words of command:

I am a black pastor in Halifax, Nova Scotia from a very mixed background. Some of my ancestors were escaped slaves from America who, during the American War of

Independence, emigrated as Loyalists to settle in Nova Scotia. Others were slaves marooned from their slave ships. Still others were Aztec Indians who came as slaves on the trade ships that brought goods to Halifax.

I became a Christian in 1982. I had my own successful carpentry business until 1990, when interest rates skyrocketed and I went through bankruptcy. This was a very hard time for me. Having lost everything except my family and my faith, I felt so ashamed for having failed. I felt like I was in a desert – empty and void of hope for the future. Needing his help and comfort, I cried out to God to come to me and restore me.

In February of 1991, the kingdom of God broke through to me at a conference where John White was speaking on his book, *When the Spirit Comes with Power*.[9] On Saturday morning, for some reason, he spoke about a butterfly's wings being strengthened as it breaks out of a cocoon. I expected to see a butterfly that cold winter morning as something was stirring within me. Saturday afternoon he spoke again about the Spirit and asked us to get into groups and pray because the Spirit was going to come in power. The worship leader began playing his guitar and then speaking about being in a desert and the hand of God coming in the form of a cloud.

Well, I saw that hand coming toward me and it landed on me. It felt like my whole body was plugged into an electric outlet as deep groans erupted from the depths of my being. I wept and groaned uncontrollably, unable to move, with a battle going on within me.

---

[9]John White, *When the Spirit Comes with Power* (Downer's Grove, Illinois: IVP, 1988).

My pastor finally came over to me, looked me in the eyes and commanded the spirit of slavery to leave me. It felt like someone took a hook and pulled it through my body, up and out from the depths of my whole being. Next he commanded a spirit of shame, a "boy" spirit, and two others that I can't remember. The last one was a "nigger" spirit. When the last one left, I felt like a butterfly: "Free at last, thank God Almighty! Free at last!" The kingdom of God had come to me and now I knew I would be able to be who God created me to be. More than twelve years later, I am still walking in that freedom!

Even a relatively short time of deliverance prayer (for example, one afternoon prayer session, as described above) feels much different and more difficult than an abbreviated paragraph can convey. Often the demonic "cords" of influence and control are wound deep within a person's very identity and self-perception – perhaps generational in nature. "Sweeping the house clean" (Luke 11:24–26) may not only be difficult but, in the longer run, not very helpful. We want to avoid a fixation on "having to get them all out" immediately.

We must remember that our ultimate goal is not simply to rescue people out of one kingdom. It is also to bring them successfully into the next. Just as God did not lead his people out of Egypt to have them flounder on the shores of the Red Sea, we are not only reaching for short-lived, temporary freedom. Our emphasis is to facilitate the individual's partnering with the grace of God, so that their identity and will are strengthened and empowered, as well as their confidence in God and their ability to resist the enemy. What good is it to provide a momentary freedom that the one ministered to cannot sustain? For this reason, truly setting a person free involves a longer process of helping them grow in the strength and desire to draw near to God so that he may draw near to them.

Joy and I (along with many others in our first church plant) learned this lesson powerfully through coaching a friend on her long walk to freedom. Here is a brief retelling of her story from her perspective:

As long as I can remember, I have been very sensitive to the spiritual world. I can see now that it is part of God's generous gift to me. For many years, however, it felt more like a curse. What God intended for good, Satan usurped control over and used to harass me for many years. I experienced both physical and sexual abuse while still a young child. This so traumatized me that it opened many doors for the demonic to gain inroads into my life. I felt, as many abuse victims do, that it was entirely my fault. I also felt powerless to prevent the "abusing" spirits that in-creasingly began to harass me. Eventually these spirits exercised greater and more frequent control over me physically – sometimes virtually blinding me.

By the time I was a young mom, this oppression became unbearable. I would frequently be visited by "molesting" spirits during the day (and especially during times of worship). I had to battle to retain control of my own physical responses and I fought incessantly the fear of literally being killed. At one time, I was taking up to sixty Tylenol a day simply to cope with the constant pain that I experienced. When I came to the Vineyard, I was unable to worship. The spirits would blind and choke me until I felt like I was in a foreign place surrounded by a circle of demons threatening me. During that time of greatest discouragement, some people made a commitment to walk with me through the dark valleys that I was facing.

At first, I was somewhat tentative. I had undergone one or two classic "deliverance" sessions previously and was very discouraged by the result. The demons only "left" for the moment and crowded back once the "ministry" was over while I felt very beaten up by the process. The prayer only seemed to reinforce my helplessness and I had difficulty visualizing myself as having any identity apart from these evil forces. Thankfully, the people who committed to pray and journey with me took a very different approach.

At the outset, they explained that the goal of our prayer went far beyond simply getting demons to leave – the end result we were working toward was my eventual freedom, not only to resist the devil, but also to choose God. That, they said, would mean reconstructing my sense of personal identity as one made in the image of God, who could make meaningful choices.

I had no idea just how long the process would be. This was probably the grace of God: It took five and a half years before I was able to worship God freely! The method that they used was dramatically different to what I had experienced.[10] They didn't allow the demons to express themselves but kept them quieted "on the side-

---

[10]This model of deliverance is explained more fully in a tape series that I have produced on the topic of Spiritual Warfare. Information on how to order this tape series is available in the Resource section of the Vineyard Canada website, www.vineyard.ca.

lines", as it were, while we listened to God together. They worked with me as we followed the Holy Spirit's leading, bringing each stronghold he identified to the cross. We would deal with the underlying "holds" that gave the demons their strength. Then they would support me as I told the demon to leave me alone. Finally, we would invite God's Spirit to fill me and take control of that area.

In no ministry times did we try to "get them all". Instead we tried to determine the Holy Spirit's order and accomplish each time what he gave us the grace to accomplish. After each prayer time, they would support me as I began to walk in new ways, to establish a pattern of choosing God in that area rather than simply being a victim as before.

At first, it was very discouraging still to sense demonic oppression in the days after a time of prayer. Soon, though, this discouragement changed to a growing excitement. I could tell that I was actually gaining ground with more and more freedom! I was not being harassed in the same old areas. Instead, my battle was around different issues. I was actually getting stronger through the ongoing battle, not weaker!

When the day finally came that I was able to worship freely, I had the confidence of knowing that with God's strengthening, I could resist the devil, just like others. I could draw close to God when attacked and the devil really would flee from me. At first, I wanted nothing other than to be "normal", just like everyone else. I didn't want to have any sensitivity to the spiritual world at all. God did far more than I could have asked for. He redeemed this spiritual gift so that now I am able to say no to Satan's invitation, while allowing God to show me what he wants me to see.

I'll never forget when he first opened my eyes to see what was really happening when I was being harassed. I finally discovered why the demons had never been able to kill me. Inside the circle of taunting demonic figures, I saw, for the first time, the protective ring of angels who were keeping me safe in God's hands. I never looked back!

The beginning of this story took place approximately twenty years ago. Today our friend is not only continuing to walk in freedom; she has become a mature follower of Jesus who is being wonderfully used by him to help rescue others from similar "black holes". Positive fruit from her own courageous journey is being reaped in the lives of her family as well as many others who have been touched by her. This is the kind of freedom that Jesus has planned for all of us – nothing less!

READING THE WORDS, DOING THE WORKS

DISCUSS IT

Have you had any experience in praying for those oppressed by the demonic?

- Share briefly.
- Have any of these experiences left you discouraged, disillusioned or jaded? Share briefly.

Are there ways that you have been influenced by Satan's deception?

- Has that resulted in separation from God in any way?
- Is there any bondage that has come to you as a result of the deception and separation?

DO IT

Keep your eyes open this week for people seeking freedom from bondage.

- Share with them the Good News you have read in Chapter 5.
- Be open to pray for them.
- Also be open to journey with them long term if that is what they need.

PRAY ABOUT IT

- Pray for one another using your authority given by Jesus, if something has come to mind during the discussion time.
- Rather than demon hunting or pouncing on someone in your group, allow the person to come forward for prayer as seen in the story of the Gerasene man.

THINK ABOUT IT

The stories of liberation show how the kingdom is about spiritual warfare – about God's rule coming against the power of darkness. Your involvement on God's side changes everything. Imagine how living out this truth could change your life.

CHAPTER 6

THE KEY TO PERSEVERING

The call to follow Jesus is a call to participate with him in this divine rescue: Helping people along a journey out of the bondage of Satan's kingdom into the joyous freedom of God's rule. The rescued become the rescuers. This, as Dallas Willard would say, is the only biblical category of Christians. They are intentional apprentices of Jesus, desiring both to learn how to live appropriately under God's rule and how to offer its blessings to others.

Our place in this world is both ambassadorial and prophetic. To some extent we are already "strangers" here (1 Peter 2:11), as our citizenship is established in the next age (Ephesians 2:19–20). Our present purpose in what is, essentially, a hostile world, is to announce prophetically God's invitation in word and deed.

OUR KINGDOM MESSAGE IS OPPOSED

This announcement of another King and kingdom does not go unopposed. The kingdom message is always countercultural; it is a call to all earthly "kingdoms" to submit to the rule of the King. In this sense, our role is like that of Moses in his day. We are to confront the spiritual "pharaohs" that desire to keep God's created ones in captivity and say: "This is what the LORD, the God of Israel, says: 'Let my people go'" (Exodus 5:1). That is certainly the sense of the disciples' prayer: "May your kingdom come soon. May your will be done here on earth, just as it is in heaven" (Matthew 6:10).

Learning how to live out this kingdom mission practically is our lifelong struggle.[1] Much of the challenge is simply learning to "do what is right, to love mercy, and to walk humbly with [our] God" (Micah 6:8). It is tackling head-on the "camel" issues of Scripture (Matthew 23:23–24), those things which are, on the one hand, so easy to overlook, yet are central to God's will and heart – issues of justice, compassion, forgiveness, generosity and faithfulness. Perhaps the

---

[1] Peter Davids writes: "While we in Vineyard have embraced the kingdom story, we have embraced the version as told by G.E. Ladd thirty years ago and applied it mostly to the issues of why we should be doing the deeds of Jesus and why our success rate in doing them is not 100%. In most other aspects of our theology, we have taken over typical Evangelical theology (or, in some cases, Charismatic theology). Now at the stage when our movement developed, this was a major step forward. It was indeed a third wave of the Spirit. But a step, even a major step, does not make a journey. The road goes ever onward or, to change the metaphor, the wave rolls on beyond us. What we need to do now, is to embrace living the teaching of Jesus (not just doing the deeds) and to appropriate the updates of the kingdom story (e.g. the version told by N.T. Wright) that show how countercultural, or counter-this-age, the teaching and symbolic actions of Jesus really were. Then we need to apply it consistently to all of our community life. What might this look like? How could a full embrace of the kingdom story make us a community effectively apprenticed to our King?" ("Who Is for the King?" in the Fall 2004 edition of *Vineline* – Boots to Our Roots: Rediscovering Kingdom Theology. The *Vineline* can be viewed online at www.vineyard.ca.)

greatest power encounters take place when we resist the lure of materialism, speak out against global economic oppression or reject the subtleties of pluralism.

THE IMPORTANCE OF POWER ENCOUNTERS

These are all issues that Jesus strongly opposed in his practice and teaching. Yet, in addition to these strongholds, Jesus also confronted the tyranny of Satan evidenced in sickness and demonic oppression. Was this emphasis simply because of the relatively undeveloped state of medical science or psychological theory in the first century? I think not. I believe that seeing God's intervention in these areas is just as important today as it was in the time of Jesus.

What does Satan accomplish through physical sickness and demonic oppression? Does he not use these situations to assert his control and domination? Satan wants to proclaim that he is in firm control of this world, able to mar and disfigure God's creation as violently and randomly as he wishes. To the degree that the heavens seem closed and our earthly realities appear to be subject to the capricious malice of the evil one, we are all left in a state of intimidation and hopelessness.

Satan, recognizing his own perilous state (he doesn't control the keys to his own dungeon – Revelation 1:18), tries to ensure that his prisoners don't have sufficient hope to try the door. He will do anything he can to demonstrate that he is effectively in control and able to do whatever he wants to the human race. Hebrews 2:15 speaks of Jesus' intention to "deliver those who have lived all their lives as slaves to the fear of dying". Satan wants to paralyze us with fear of what he can do to us, so that we don't dare step out of line to incur his wrath. We "go with the flow"; unfortunately, the flow is leading us to destruction.

A large part of Jesus' public teaching and ministry involved exposing this lie and restoring hope and faith to an oppressed people. Luke records such a situation in 5:17–26. Jesus was teaching in a very crowded room (this was at the height of his visibility, attracting many religious leaders who came to examine his credibility). While he was teaching, Jesus was aware that the power of God to heal was present powerfully in the room. When a group of men cut a hole in the roof to lower a paralyzed man into the room to reach him, Jesus was not surprised. He saw great faith and expectation in these men.

Directed by God's Spirit (as he invariably was), he said something astonishing. "Your sins are forgiven," he assured the man. The religious leaders, probably already upset by the ceiling debris that had fallen on their front row seats, were incensed. Forgiveness of sins was reserved for God alone. In effect, Jesus was equating himself with God. Jesus, having the distinct advantage of being able to discern their thoughts, asked a simple question: "Is it easier to say, 'Your sins are forgiven' or 'Get up and walk'?"

Jesus' audience knew that, on one level, unless God came near and touched the man, both would be impossible. Only God could heal either the body or the spirit. On the other hand, it certainly was easier to say, "Get up and walk!" The spiritual could remain invisible, only to be seen on judgment day; the physical would be immediately visible. Jesus turned to the paralyzed man and said: "Stand up, take your mat, and go on home." When the man jumped to his feet, long-dormant hope leaped in the hearts of physically and spiritually oppressed. If Jesus could free physical paralysis, truly the age to come was within reach with its promised liberation in all dimensions of life.

This is why we must proclaim to the sick and demonized: "The kingdom of God is within your reach! God's deliverance is not beyond your ability to grasp it. Satan's domination is not so secure or extensive that your situation is hopeless. In fact, the kingdom is already upon us all and our salvation is at hand!" Every time we cast out a demon or pray for physical sickness or injury, we are making this statement of faith: Though in some ways it is delayed, the rule of God has come and will come and the gates of hell will not be able to prevent its fulfilment. Every time a body is healed, every time a life is freed, the spell of Satan's despair is weakened, the crack in the door to his dungeon is widened and light streams in.

When we pray, we are reaching for the kingdom and proclaiming that it is within reach. If I don't see it today, I may tomorrow or the following day. If I cannot pray from faith, I pray from hope. When I am relatively hopeless, I pray out of principle – the strong man has been fatally wounded and his time is short. I have been commissioned to take the plunder (Luke 11:21–22; Matthew 28:18–20).

THE MYSTERY OF THE KINGDOM

It is one thing to rise in faith for a single occasion, but quite another to remain faithful for a lifetime. When we encounter the kingdom, it is easy to be motivated. When the disciples and the crowds saw Jesus' miraculous works, it was easy to believe that the end was immanent. Similarly, when our prayers are working and we are seeing healings, deliverance and miracles, we are euphoric. Yet that euphoria is inevitably tempered over time by another kingdom reality, the already/not yet (the delay of the kingdom). This was the "mystery" or "secret" of the kingdom that Jesus shared with his closest disciples (Matthew 13:11). What Jesus brought was certainly God's kingdom, yet it would not come in complete fulfilment. It would be rejected by some, it would even suffer violence (resulting in Jesus' death); the present evil age would continue to exist alongside it.

The disciples did not fully understand that the delay of full judgment was necessary for the time of invitation and mercy that God wanted to accomplish through Jesus' suffering and death, so that many more could be welcomed into friendship with him. They lived and died in the reality of a mixture of two ages. Paul experienced times of tremendous success (Acts 19:11–12), yet he also had times of great despair (2 Corinthians 1:8–9; 12:8–10; Philippians 2:27).

This can be very confusing for us and severely tests the depth of our commitment to our kingdom commission. My greatest crisis of commitment did not come in the early days of learning to pray for the sick – at that stage I was quite patient, expecting that it might take some time to "learn the ropes". My most difficult times took place later, after witnessing some very powerful interventions of God. I had seen him heal blindness, deafness, cancer and many other serious illnesses through my prayers. Yet I became increasingly frustrated and discouraged, almost to the point of wanting to quit entirely.

How could that be? The pain of what *didn't* happen

through my prayers overwhelmed me. I saw people healed of cancer; but at the same time some of my best friends died from it in spite of my best prayers. I experienced the supernatural gift of faith miraculously to stop the miscarriage of our daughter. Yet many years later, I agonized in prayer over that same daughter, reaching for that faith to no avail as she lost her beautiful baby boy at a similar stage of pregnancy.

I couldn't bear the tension of the already/not yet. Before I accepted this commission, I could simply stay away from painful situations. Now I found myself in the worst place of all: My heart would engage, but I couldn't guarantee a result. Even worse than the fact that only some would be healed was the acknowledgement that I couldn't choose which ones it would be. I found anger toward God building up in me. According to my perspective, he seemed to choose to release his grace to all the wrong people.

At other times, God would intervene miraculously but incompletely. I struggled to see his goodness in those situations. He spoke prophetically to dear friends of Joy's and mine about a son who would be given to them at a specific time – one who would help his father in his work. When the time came, their son was born – with serious mental handicaps that would make him dependent on them for the rest of their lives.

Recently, in our home church, a woman shared a powerful encounter she had with Jesus approximately nine years ago. At the time she was far from God – other than some Sunday School experience as a little girl, she was completely unchurched, having embraced the hippie culture with its associated lifestyle. The crisis that precipitated this encounter was the birth of her first child (a girl), who was significantly premature and, as a result, had suffered massive brain haemorrhaging. Because she was not expected to live more than a few hours, the mother decided to spend that time in the intensive care nursery with her dying child, holding her hand until she passed on.

In that distraught place, she cried out to the Jesus she remembered from her Sunday School experience. "I really need you right now," she cried, pouring out her heart and repenting of all the bad decisions she had made in her life. At one point in that process, she felt a hand on her shoulder. When she turned her head to look, it was a real hand connected to a figure completely bathed in an overpowering white light. Somehow she knew that it was Jesus! She experienced a power that came into her from Jesus and went through her into her dying child. Immediately, all her vital signs became normal. By the next morning, her child was breathing on her own and was removed from life-support. The doctors still believed that she would die within a few days. Nine years later, she is still very much alive – a testimony to the amazing intervention of God. Nine years later, she is also significantly challenged mentally and physically. How could this be? How could God come with such power and save her from certain death, yet leave her in need of constant care?

This is the mystery of the kingdom: It has come and it is yet to come. We have tasted the powers of the coming age, yet we are still touched by the destructive evil of this present one. This eschatological tension is a difficult one to live in and I understand the desire to escape it. I understand the triumphalist desire to have it all now, believing that we need to seize the promises of God expressed through Jesus. The taste of the age to come is tantalizing and it is tempting to seek a system that will guarantee the full banquet now. "Strike up the battle sounds, let's seize the day!" Unfortunately, the wounded must be shot; there is no place for a theology of suffering. To acknowledge any continued expression of this present evil age is construed as weakness and unbelief.

I also understand the tendency to take control and break the tension in the opposite direction, relegating promises for healing and deliverance to the next age, after this life. We suck it up, carry one another and pray for grace to endure the sufferings of this life – our reward comes in the next. At least there is a sense of control and protection from disappointment.

It is easier to believe for what we cannot see than it is to hope for change in what we can. Yet we are called to hope and faith in the midst of this tension. Until Jesus returns to bring into fulfilment the reign of God in this world, our lives will always be marked by the conflict between good and evil. This is a real conflict, with real casualties and setbacks – the cost of delayed judgment. Yet there is also great reward as mercy triumphs over judgment. We catch glimpses of true life and freedom that fix our eyes and sustain us in our journey in this "time between the times".

IS MORE POWER THE KEY?

If this is our present kingdom reality, how can we not only endure but also thrive? Our first thought is: "Give us more power, Lord!" At least we want to ensure that the proportion of "already" relative to "not yet" is a healthy one. We are prepared to cope with a limited amount of trial and suffering, as long as we are assured that the preponderance of our experience is marked by supernatural intervention. And the key to that outcome is more spiritual power. If the tension cannot be entirely broken in this age, we at least want it considerably "bent" in our favour.

Perhaps Jesus' first disciples felt much the same. On their return from their first ministry trip without Jesus (Luke 10:1–20), they were elated at the fact that power had flowed through them just as they had seen it being released through Jesus. "Lord, even the demons obey us when we use your name!" they exclaimed with obvious excitement. They no doubt understood that power would be the key to their success.

Jesus' response was somewhat surprising. It almost seemed like he dumped cold water on their parade. After acknowledging that their victory had supernatural as well as natural implications and that they could expect more of the same, he quenched their exuberance with the caution: "But don't rejoice just because evil spirits obey you; rejoice because your names are registered as citizens of heaven."

What was Jesus trying to say? Was he jealous because the disciples were enjoying the same kind of success that he had experienced? Of course not! The whole intention of their apprenticeship was to bring them to this place. It had always been his purpose to leave them doing what he had been doing. What was he trying to say?

First, he was not trying to discourage the presence of God's power in their discipleship. God wants our life and discipleship to be marked by evidences of his power working in and through us. This early trip was just a prequel of what God promised would be the norm for their lives. "But when the Holy Spirit has come upon you, you will receive power and will tell people about me everywhere" (Acts 1:8). The story of the expanding early church is filled with illustrations of God's Spirit powerfully expressing his active presence in and through it. This same power is constantly evidenced in the church throughout its history to the present day. There are ebbs and flows, times when that presence and power is more or less received and experienced, but in every age, there is a thread of the original promise being realized.

Rather than simply muting their enthusiasm over the power they had experienced, Jesus was trying to help the disciples understand that, exciting as this victory was, one battle does not a war make. Jesus wasn't just committed to a short-term win; he was dedicated to them ultimately winning the war against Satan. If they were to accomplish this, they would need to understand the difference between authority and power. He had not sent them out into a battle of power against power; he had sent them out with ambassadorial authority.

POWER AND AUTHORITY

What is the difference between these terms? Are power and authority not interchangeable? Let's examine both to see the significant difference in meaning. Power is, quite simply, the ability to perform or act effectively, particularly with strength or force. There was a time, when my son was young, when I had power over him. I loved to play a game of arm wrestling with him, sometimes with the assistance of his younger sister. They would both gang up on my arm to see if they could pull it over. I, of course, would play along, with much groaning and apparent consternation, feigning defeat. At the last moment, however, I would smile at them, and with ease snap my arm over – winning the day and re-asserting the fact that Dad was indeed the ultimate power in our tiny universe.

This went on for years until the day, in my son's mid-teens, when I once again invited him to a "friendly" arm wrestle. He readily agreed and things went along as scripted until the decisive moment: I grinned, applied ultimate pressure against his resisting arm and … nothing happened! His arm didn't move. It was a stalemate. A slight smile played at the corners of his mouth as his eyes caught mine and we both knew what had happened. I no longer had power over my son. (We never arm wrestled again – I was happy to end my career with a tie.)

All power is ultimately God's. "All glory … majesty, power, and authority belong to him, in the beginning, now, and forevermore," writes Jude (v. 25). God "was" before any created thing; everything owes its continued existence to him alone (Colossians 1:17). He is the sole Creator; no other power exists in this universe but his. Power can only be exercised where God either delegates or allows it. Satan can only exist as he "usurps" and illicitly uses God's power (he is, as we have previously noted, God's devil).

Authority is somewhat different. It is the right to use power. As the Creator and Sustainer of all that is, God is not only the ultimate power, but also the supreme authority. He alone determines what is authorized use of his power. That does not mean that unauthorized use of his power is not possible; it does, however, mean that all such use will have consequences for the usurper – everyone pays the piper in

God's universe. Unlike Satan, who ultimately will pay for his unauthorized use of God's power, we have been given authority explicitly to extend God's kingdom. In Luke 10, Jesus is simply reminding his disciples that he authorized them to overturn Satan's work when he first called them (Mark 3:14–15). In his final commission before he left for heaven, he officially sent them out to extend the kingdom by making disciples, a commission that clearly applies to us today (Matthew 28:18–20).

The key understanding, however, for both the first disciples and for us, is to know just how this authority functions. Is it a promise from God to make us more powerful than his enemy? Is it a commitment to make us demigods that need not be afraid of our spiritual opposition? This is precisely *not* how authority is to operate in us. As Paul clarifies in his letters, our authoritative role is similar to that of an ambassador.

Ambassadors have very little direct power but, depending on the nation they represent, they may have great authority. The American ambassador to Canada, for instance, does not come with an army. Even our limited armed forces could, if we chose, overpower the American embassy and capture their ambassador. The consequences for Canada, however, would be significant. The American ambassador has great authority. As long as he is fulfilling the wishes and directives of the government that has authorized him, he speaks and acts with their full backing. If anyone opposes him, they must deal with the full power of the sovereign state that has sent him. Anyone who harms the ambassador will suffer the consequences.

As I was attempting to understand this concept, my

mind went back to the period of my life when I was a young, developing adult. I was very concerned about power. I grew up in a rough neighbourhood and had the distinct disadvantage of always being the smallest in my class. Fortunately, during my ninth year at school, I grew significantly (about ten inches in a year). Unfortunately, I didn't manage to gain any weight. This state of affairs, combined with the fact that I had unusually large lips at the time (my lips were born and I kind of grew up around them) created a rather comical caricature (picture lips on a stick)! Of course, it was comical primarily to everyone else – to me it was a tragedy. I was consumed with changing this state of affairs.

During this time, I was quite taken with a cartoon advertisement that used to appear regularly in various magazines. The purpose was to highlight how the Charles Atlas exercise program could change your life.[2] Each cartoon strip followed the same script. It always began with a skinny young man (that I always identified with) that miraculously had the most beautiful girlfriend. Often he would make the same grievous mistake: He would take her to the beach. ("No, don't do it!" I would caution – he never listened.) Invariably, they would be confronted by a buff, powerful man (on steroids?), who would kick sand in the young man's face and humiliate him in front of his girlfriend. Discouraged, he would walk away, only to discover the magazine ad. Immediately he would send away for this extraordinary secret program and, within minutes of receiving it and putting it into practice, he would be transformed into the ultimate specimen of macho manhood. With new confidence, he would head for the beach and impress the

---

[2]http://www.charlesatlas.com.

girl by asserting his newfound power. ("She's bad news," I warned, but he still never listened.)

This is a classic example of power over power. Often we approach our kingdom commission just that way, looking for the magic program that will transform us into "men and women of power", who will be able to overpower our evil opponents single-handedly. How could this story be changed to illustrate the true nature of our commission, that of ambassadorial authority?

I suppose the story might play out much the same way until the young man wanders despondently away from the beach. This time, however, he doesn't encounter a magazine advertisement; he runs into an old friend – Arnold Schwarzenegger. As he pours out his heart to Arnie, his friend says, "Let's go back and right this wrong!" Excitedly, our young man returns, finds the beach bully and, puffing up his chest, announces, "You're outta here!" With a frightened stare, the man forgets all about the beautiful girl and literally races for safety! Who is he staring at? At first it might appear that he is looking at our new hero. In reality, he is looking just past him to the one riding shotgun off his right shoulder – Arnold! "Hasta la vista, baby!" he says. This is authority over power. Our man hasn't gained a pound or grown an inch. He has, however, gained authorization from a superior power that has agreed to "back his act".

This kind of support can be intoxicating. I can imagine our young man becoming so zealous that he decides to rid the beach of every undesirable. This could work well ... until Arnold breaks for lunch or decides that the mission has now exceeded what he originally "authorized". So it is with our kingdom mission. Our success is commensurate to the authority that backs us and that backing is totally dependent on our obedience. When we are simply walking out what we have been commissioned to do, we can expect God's support.

THE AUTHORITY OF JESUS

This kind of authority was the defining characteristic of Jesus' ministry. What caused him to stand out were not impressive physical characteristics. Isaiah prophesied that this would not be the case (Isaiah 53:2). What both people and demons recognized about him was that he seemed to be supported by the full force of heaven. When he spoke, it sounded like God was speaking (Mark 1:21–22); when he encountered demonic powers, they surrendered (Mark 1:27). He even had authority over the forces of nature (Mark 4:41)! What was Jesus' explanation for this unprecedented authority? He explained that he always acted in complete submission to his Father's heart and will (John 5:19–20; 6:38; 8:28–29; 12:50).

Jesus understood clearly the importance of this absolute submission. As a man, he would be vulnerable if he allowed any opportunity for Satan to separate him from complete unity with his Father. The whole redemptive mission depended on uncompromised obedience to God's will. Satan's strategy was to lure him into the same kind of separation that had been so effective in the garden (Luke 4:1–13). Jesus refused to be drawn into any kind of independent action. He countered every temptation from within authority rather than with power. "The Scriptures say …" was his only response.

AUTHORITY, NOT POWER, IS TO BE
THE PATTERN FOR JESUS' DISCIPLES

We have much to learn from Jesus' example, as did his first disciples. Power, whether physical or spiritual, is a dangerous commodity. Some years ago, I ran into a friend who was an electrician and was shocked to see a large wound on his hand. It looked as though something had literally eaten away part of it, leaving a gaping hole. Seeing my shocked response, he explained that he had been working on a job that required the power to be left on. He was making some careful adjustments next to a line that carried six hundred volts of electricity. Despite all his caution, his hand slipped and touched the live wire. As it did so, the electricity began to eat away his flesh. "I simply couldn't pull my hand away," he explained. "The power held me." Only the grace of God, as he cried out to him, suddenly released him. He was left with a vivid reminder of the danger of power.

What is true in the physical is true of the spiritual. If we touch too much power, too long, it begins to hold us – until it literally destroys us. It is addictive. Humans were never meant to handle it. Satan is not frightened by "powerful" people. Although his illicit use of God's power is destroying him, he is an expert at using it similarly to destroy the lives of others. It is foolhardy to think that we will have the wisdom and skill to use God's power (even on his behalf) to outsmart and defeat that cunning serpent, the devil.

Jesus was emphasizing to his disciples on their return from their powerful ministry experience the focus that he himself modelled: "My promise to you has not been power over power, but authority over power." Don't become enamoured or enticed by power, even for noble purposes.

The key to ultimate victory is your right to appeal to the Father's actions on your behalf, and the key to this authorization is submitted relationship – being assured that "your names are registered as citizens of heaven" (Luke 10:20).

That which Jesus knew and passed on to his disciples is critically important for us. The real answer to the spiritual warfare in which we find ourselves is not power or "anointing"; it is the Spirit of the Anointed One living within us. God's desire is for us to battle his enemy from the safety of his authority, keeping the power necessary for victory in his hands. That is the only safe place from which such power can be exercised.

THE WEAKNESS OF AUTHORITY

From a human perspective, such a process seems very weak. We prefer approaches built on our ability and desire for control. Perhaps it betrays our preference to trust in ourselves rather than rely on God: We are more drawn to being generals than ambassadors. I'm sure the apostle Paul had similar struggles. In 2 Corinthians 12:7 he speaks of a "thorn in his flesh", sent from Satan to torment and discourage him. (We cannot be sure whether this was a physical affliction or the harassment from Judaizing elements responsible for his constant persecution.) Three times he begged God to remove it. No doubt he argued with God about how effective he could be without this constant opposition.

What was God's response? Three times he said: "My gracious favour is all you need. My power works best in your weakness" (12:9). Eventually, though, Paul came to the place of understanding the great strength of weakness:

When we are weak, we are dependent; when we are dependent, we stay close to the source of our protection. As a result, we never lack for power (God is quick to supply the power necessary to accomplish his purposes), but we don't have to fear being deceived or controlled by it – the power stays in God's hands. Paul actually got to the place where the thing he boasted about was his weaknesses. He saw them as the key to unlocking tremendous power from God exercised on his behalf. When persecution and hardship pressed in on him, rather than becoming discouraged or anxious, he let them drive him to God. Through this paradoxical process, weakness became the key to continued strength.

This principle of authority is wonderfully illustrated in the response of the early church to the persecution they endured from both religious and political leaders (Acts 4). When Peter and John were freed after being threatened, they returned to the believers and shared the ultimatum they had been given: "Never again share in this name of Jesus or the full power of our regimes will be brought against you!"

Their response is a classic demonstration of authority. They immediately cried out to God, drawing near to him. "O Lord," they prayed, "hear their threats ..." (4:29). What they asked for next, however, is not power but courage – courage to do what Jesus had commissioned them to do. They understood that the heavenly role (dealing with the principalities and powers that lay behind and empowered these persecutors) was God's role. Their part was to trust God and obey what he had asked them to do. Their primary request was: "Help us, Lord, to be the faithful ambassadors that you desire us to be."

Second, they made an additional appeal. "As we obey," they said, "would you send your power, confronting the enemy's kingdom just as you did with Pharaoh. Let us see the signs that mark your kingdom coming!" They were content to remain weak, but appealed to God to be strong on their behalf. The ensuing chapters record both their faithfulness and God's with the result that God's kingdom powerfully advanced in very visible ways.

We all long to see personally and experience the seemingly "instant" results alluded to in Acts 5:12–16. Yet the way in which God chooses to demonstrate his power and will, may often seem very natural. While instantaneous "miracles" are far more appealing, God frequently uses our prayers to release a process of healing. Only in the longer term do we see the power of God at work.

John Wimber taught me to celebrate both ways of God accomplishing his healing work. Many times I saw people healed at the very moment of his prayer. When such results did not occur, however, John never seemed to lose enthusiasm or commitment. Even in situations where we saw no discernible response to our prayers, he would stay focused on God's desire and ability to heal. How it happened didn't matter to John. He was as content to see God working through medical means as he was to see more dramatic visitations of healing. He simply tried to remain faithful to Jesus' instruction to "always pray and never give up" (Luke 18:1).

One of the last people John prayed for before his own death was a young boy named Zachari, son of a Canadian worship leader named Andrew Smith and his wife Tami, who was suffering from terminal cancer. I was with John when he prayed for Zach the second time. Nothing seemed to happen during the prayer, but I know that John cared deeply about this boy's future and continued to pray for Zach during the last months of his own life. During the opportunities that John had to pray for Zach, there were no observable gifts of power – none of us saw any evidence of a healing gift being released. The only gift that John Wimber (the internationally known and highly anointed healer) received was an insight about vegetables.[3] Zach's mother Tami tells the story:

> Zach got sick in November 1994 and by the time they diagnosed him with K1 Lymphoma, he was filled with tumours and covered with cancerous bruises. He was at death's door. Our family (Andrew and I and our three daughters) moved to Vancouver for Zach's intensive chemotherapy. Our church community rallied around us in practical ways and intense prayer support.
>
> After five months of intensive chemotherapy – the most chemo they had given to any child at the Vancouver Children's Hospital – we returned to Kelowna, praying for the best. John Wimber prayed for Zach that spring. John was praying for more healing (when we thought it was over). John felt that diet was important for Zach's healing and saw a picture of celery and carrots.
>
> Zach relapsed, as the doctors would say, in early June and was now diagnosed with a tumour in his head. We began more chemo treatments and radiation to the

---

[3]After the first prayer time, John shared with me that he believed Zach would struggle greatly for a period of time but would thrive by his mid-teens. He also believed that diet would be a significant factor in his healing.

brain. The only medical hope for a cure after this second round of treatment was a bone marrow transplant. The doctors didn't offer much hope that it would be successful. At this point Zach was having violent reactions to the chemo, and his body couldn't take any more.

We went home to pray about the bone marrow transplant with the understanding there was no suitable donor and that there was only a slim possibility of this being a cure. At the same time, this was our last medical hope. We agonized that September and finally decided to put his fate and future in God's hands, accepting that God might want to take him. The doctors understood our decision and suggested we get a live-in nurse and take him home and prepare for him to die. As parents, we were fighting for our sanity.

We lived on pins and needles for two months and promised ourselves that if Zach were still with us at the end of the year, we would take him with Andrew and his band on a tour of Sweden. On our return in late January, instead of waiting for Zach to die, we began to walk slowly out from under the cloud of death. Zach got stronger and stronger.

We met with John Wimber in the fall of that year. He asked how Zach was and said he still prayed for him. He asked for a picture of Zach to put on his fridge at home. We told him we took his advice about celery and carrots and Zach had a very healthy diet of organic food. The next day John said he was praying for Zach that night and felt that carrots and green leafy vegetables were a part of his healing.

To this day, ten years later, we still meet people

around the world who had heard about Zach and his trial, have persevered in praying for him and wonder how he is doing. The doctors told us that Zach would suffer hearing loss and some brain damage. Instead, Zach has recovered completely and only suffers with minor joint pain when he plays sports. He is a wonderful person, an excellent musician and student, and will graduate this year.

"I have given you authority over all the power of the enemy ..." (Luke 10:19). What great news for us today! It means that doing the works of Jesus, even his supernatural ones, isn't dependent on our great anointing, charisma or personal power. We don't have to keep pumping ourselves up (and everyone else around us) until we are addicted to spiritual adrenalin. We can be naturally supernatural because we have been given an anointed, empowered task – the Great Commission. When we put our hands to it, the hands of Jesus join with us. "Be sure of this," he says, "I am with you always, even to the end of the age" (Matthew 28:20). Who would want it any other way?

READING THE WORDS, DOING THE WORKS

DISCUSS IT

As you have read and practised these six chapters,

- Share what you have learned with the others in your group.
- Spend time together thanking the Father for his graciousness. (Remember to be just as excited about others' answers to prayer as your own!)

What opposition have you faced to keep you from persevering?

- Share with your partner.

Gary uses the Charles Atlas illustration to show the difference between power and authority.

- Can you think of other useful illustrations to demonstrate this difference?

Examine the circles of influence that God has given you.

- This can be in your home, workplace or church.
- Can you think of a current situation in which you are feeling "powerless"? Share honestly.

DO IT

We all love to be in control.

- This week, when you are in a situation where you are tempted to use power plays, consciously surrender the situation to the guidance of the Lord.
- Ask God to give you the determination to walk into any situation into which he calls you with courage, relying on his strength and ability to give you authority, rather than relying on your own abilities and power.

PRAY ABOUT IT

This is a prayer that Gary and I feel is to be prayed for our lifetime. We invite you to pray it with us:

Dear Father, we long to see your kingdom come to this world as many times and in as many ways as possible during our lifetime. We ask for healing, deliverance, salvation and the dead to be raised. We choose to plant as many seeds as we can in our lifetime, so that the crop you harvest will last for eternity.

Knowing this will neither be quick nor easy, we ask you for the courage and strength to follow you for a lifetime. May the glory be yours!

THINK ABOUT IT

Though we may have read the words of a book, often the content needs to be worked into us with constant use. For some of us, the principles that have been talked about here may be new. The goal of this book is not just to gain more information, but to live a transformed life. Consider reading the book a second time in order to review the material and be encouraged as you continue to put it into practice.

BIBLIOGRAPHY

Bruce Collins, *Prophecy* (Berkhamstead: New Wine Publications, 2000).

Gordon Fee, *The First Epistle to the Corinthians* (Grand Rapids: William B. Eerdmans, 1987).

Bill Hybels and Mark Mittleberg, *Becoming a Contagious Christian* (Grand Rapids: Zondervan, 1996).

C.S. Lewis, *The Problem of Pain* (San Francisco: HarperSan Francisco, 2001).

Derek Morphew, *Breakthrough: Discovering the Kingdom* (Cape Town: Vineyard International Publishing, 2001).

Derek Morphew, *The Spiritual Spider Web: A Study of Ancient and Contemporary Gnosticism* (Cape Town: Vineyard Bible Institute, www.vineyardbi.org).

Mark Stibbe, *Prophetic Evangelism: When God Speaks to Those Who Don't Know Him* (Authentic Media, 2004).

John White, *When the Spirit Comes with Power* (Downers Grove, IL; IVP, 1988).

Dallas Willard, *The Divine Conspiracy: Rediscovering Our Hidden Life in God* (San Francisco: HarperSanFrancisco, 1998).

Dallas Willard, *Renovation of the Heart: Putting on the Character of Christ* (Colorado Springs: NavPress, 2002).

N.T. Wright, *The Challenge of Jesus: Rediscovering Who Jesus Was and Is* (Downers Grove, IL: InterVarsity Press, 1999).

N.T. Wright, *The New Testament and the People of God* (Minneapolis: Fortress Press, 1992).

N.T. Wright, *What Saint Paul Really Said* (Grand Rapids: William B. Eerdmans, 1977).

John Howard Yoder, *The Politics of Jesus* (Grand Rapids: William B. Eerdmans, 1994).

BOOK ORDERS

This book can be ordered from the following Vineyard International Publishing distributors:

Australia
AVC Australia
P.O. Box 652
Lilydale, VIC 3140
Fax: +03 9739 7946
Tel: +03 9739 4940
office@vineyard.org.au

Benelux
Inside Out Publishers
Postbus 2573
3800 GC Amersfoort
Fax: +31 (0)33 4559252
info@insideoutpublishers.nl

Canada
Vineyard Resource Canada
#403 19292 60th ave
Surrey, BC, V3S 3M2
Tel: +604 539-8570
naturallysupernatural@vineyard.ca

England
Ed & Clare Evans
9 Poplar Way,
Salisbury, SP1 3GR
Tel: +44 1722 326885
edevans@talk21.com

New Zealand
VMG Aotearoa NZ
116 Wairere Rd
Waitakere, Auckland, NZ
vmg-anz@vineyard.co.nz

Norway
Oslo Vineyard
St Halvardsgt.20
0192, Oslo, Norway
Tel: +47 24070707
victoria@vineyard.no

South Africa
P.O. Box 53286, Kenilworth 7745
Tel & Fax: +27 21 6712633
vip@vineyardbi.org
www.vineyardbi.org/vip

Sweden
Krister Burstrom
Din Bok i Skelleftea
Stationsgatan 12
931 31 Skelleftea
krister@dinbok.net

Switzerland
Mathew Mathai
Wehntalerstrasse 276
8046-Zurich, Switzerland
Tel: +41 1 371 7151
Fax: +41 1 371 7150
mathew@vineyard.ch

USA
Vineyard Music USA
12743 Capricorn, Suite 400
Stafford, Texas, 77477
Tel: +1 800 852 8463
sales@vineyardmusicusa.com